REDEMPTION

REDEMPTION

The Truth Behind the Michael Jackson
Child Molestation Allegations

Geraldine Hughes

B & V

Branch & Vine Publishers, LLC
Radford, VA

Branch & Vine Publishers, LLC

PO Box 1297, Radford, Virginia 24143

Redemption, copyright © 1997 & 2004 by Geraldine Hughes

All rights reserved. No part of this publication may be reproduced, stored in a retrieval system or transmitted in any way by means, electronic, mechanical, photocopy, recording or otherwise, without the prior written permission from the publisher, except as where provided by USA copyright law.

All scriptures quotations, unless otherwise indicated, are taken from the New King James Version, Copyright © 1979, 1980, 1982 by Thomas Nelson, Inc. Used by permission. All rights reserved.

Every possible effort has been explored to secure permission to reprint previously published material. However, oversights may occur and should be brought to the attention of the publisher for rectification in subsequent printing.

Branch & Vine Publishers, LLC, its employees, contractors, and vendors accepts no liability for the contents and are not responsible for the accuracy of the information contained herein.

First Edition

ISBN 1-57688-036-2

Library of Congress Control Number: 2003115809

Cover designed by Donna McNutt

Image Illustration by Jennifer Phillips Webster

Scales Illustration by Michael Zug

Printed in the United States of America

10 9 8 7 6 5 4 3 2 1

Contents

Dedication 9
Publisher's Page 11
A Note To My Readers 13
Prologue 15
1. **Introduction** 17
1.1 About the Author 22
2. **The Main Characters** 31
2.1 Rothman - The Lawyer 33
2.2 The 13-year old Boy 44
2.3 Dr. Chandler - The Father 49
2.4 David and June Schwartz .53
2.5 Pellicano - The Investigator 55
2.6 Dr. Mantis Abrams - The Psychiatrist 62
2.7 Michael Jackson - The Icon 64
3. **The Plot Thickens** 69
3.1 20 Million Dollar Demand 71
3.2 Negotiations Halted 73
3.3 The Custody Battle 76
3.4 The Surprise Motion 80
3.5 Third Party Disclosure 83
3.6 Allegations Launched 86
3.7 The Child Molestation Investigation 89

4.	**The Aftermath**	93
4.1	The Media Goes Wild	95
4.2	What Reporters Were Dying to Know	98
4.3	Secret Meetings	100
4.4	The Extortion Investigation	102
4.5	Jackson Changes Attorneys	104
4.6	The Settlement	107
5.	**Legally Speaking**	111
5.1	The Civil Lawsuit	113
5.2	The Criminal Investigation	137
5.3	Attorney / Client Privilege	140
5.4	Litigation Facts	143
6.	**A Ram In The Bush**	147
7.	**Here And Now**	157
7.1	The Fans	159
7.2	Michael Moves On With His Life	163
8.	**Afterword**	165
	Michael, The Humanitarian	171
	Appendix	177
	Spiritually Speaking	179
	Excerpts From Geraldine Hughes' Diary	182
	Excerpts From the Recorded Telephone Conversation Between Dr. Chandler and Mr. Dave Schwartz	184

REDEMPTION

The Truth Behind the Michael Jackson
Child Molestation Allegations

Dedication

This book is dedicated to my mother, who not only gave me the courage to come forth in the very beginning, but to continue my efforts in getting this book completed and published.

I would also like to thank Anthony Pellicano for his extensive investigation efforts in digging up all the facts surrounding this case.

Publisher's Page

Production of this manuscript was well under way when the latest allegations against Michael Jackson were made public. At that point we decided to move up the release date because of the sudden demand for the book. Because of this, we want to apologize to the reader for any errors in production that may have occurred.

To respect the privacy of the then 13-year old boy we have decided not to identify him by name.

My thanks to our staff for their hard work in getting this manuscript prepared on such short notice —
Editorial Department: Steven and Debra Macon, Meagen Pratt, and Connie Armentrout.
Art Department: Donna McNutt, Mike Zug and Jennifer Phillips Webster.
Marketing: Donna Bird.

James Armentrout
Chief Executive Officer,
Branch & Vine Publishers, LLC

A Note To My Readers

I originally titled this book *The Set-Up*. Defined as: To put forward (as a plan) for acceptance. Cause. Create. To make carefully worked out plans for... To come into active operation or use...

I have since decided to change the title to *Redemption* which means: To extricate from an undesirable state." In other words, "to put something back into its proper place that was taken out of place."

I want to begin by stating that I do not know Michael Jackson and I have never met Michael Jackson. I am not coming forth on behalf of anyone that knows Michael Jackson. I have not been paid by Michael Jackson nor am I acting on behalf of anyone for Michael Jackson to come forth with this book. I have not had any assistance in coming forth with this book by Michael Jackson or for anyone working on behalf of Michael Jackson.

I am coming forth on my own initiative and represent that everything written in this book is what I witnessed, is of my own belief and from my personal and public knowledge. I can attest to the truthfulness of the information contained herein.

Prologue

In the summer of 1993 I was the sole legal secretary who worked for Barry Rothman, the attorney representing the father of the 13-year old boy who accused Michael Jackson of child molestation. I am coming forth to give a truthful account of the events that led up to the child molestation allegations. I also want to shed light on the facts surrounding the case. I feel it is time for the world to know what I have known all along concerning the child molestation allegations against Michael Jackson. The truth will speak for itself.

Redemption brings leverage to the child molestation allegation since it all started with the accusations of one boy. Now, with the witness of one, I would like to present you with another point of view that will bring you the truth about the Michael Jackson child molestation allegations as I witnessed from inside the walls of the accusers's camp.

All the information contained in this book is of my own personal knowledge, based on what I witnessed and a great deal is available from public records—also upon my First Amendment rights—Freedom of Speech.

I am not divulging any information that is protected under attorney/client privilege. It is my position that the attorney/client relationship was not ethical and offers no protection based on the following: The protection which is granted to the attorney/client relationship is based upon the assumption that lawyers are consulted for the purpose of ethical and legal activity, rather than to devise means to break the law. When the fundamental trust that society places in lawyers is breached, so too is the protection that the attorney/client privilege affords, and that privilege is no longer applicable. The attorney-client privilege was designed to facilitate the administration of justice, not to thwart it.

In addition — nothing contained in this book is designed to cast a shadow of doubt on the competency of our District Attorney's office, our police departments, the Department of Children's Services, psychiatrists and/or the media. The references made in this book concerning the above mentioned agencies are referenced only to give an account of what actually transpired during the case. In no way do I wish to cast doubt regarding their competence and/or credibility.

I thank God for the many men and women who work with the District Attorney's office, the many police department agencies, the court system, the Department of Children's Services, the psychiatrists and the media. It is a joint effort on all of their parts that keep our streets safe on a day to day basis. Although I make strong comments concerning the handling of this case, I must point out that they were all operating under the belief that a crime against a child had actually been committed. While I applaud their efforts in seeking justice, it appears that many of them got caught up in the frenzy and did not want to let go when no evidence to support the allegations could be found.

Part One
Introduction

Introduction

It is now ten years after the child molestation allegations against Michael Jackson hit the news, and there are millions of people who feel the whole truth concerning the case has not yet been told. After the media hype subsided, after all the breaking news stories ceased, there still remains a sense of incompleteness concerning what happened. Usually when someone commits a crime and has two county District Attorney's offices on their trails, there is generally an arrest and the person is at least brought to trial, if not justice. Since no charges were brought against Michael Jackson, the only conclusion to this case was that the civil charge was settled out of court for an undisclosed amount of money. Since no formal charges were ever brought against Michael Jackson, there are a lot of intelligent people all over the world that believe he was shafted.

It is my position that Michael Jackson was innocent of the allegations of child molestation based on the facts I will put forth in this book. I saw behavior, heard statements and saw documents that were more consistent with someone carrying out an elaborate extortion scheme than someone trying to pursue justice.

I have been trying for ten years to get this information out to the public. During the investigation, I stepped forward and provided this information to the defense investigation team. When the case settled, the information that I provided which would have come out in a court trial, did not reach the public. I was at a loss as to how to go about getting this information out to the public's attention so they could know what I have known all along—that Michael Jackson was innocent of the allegations of child molestation.

I cannot provide hard evidence to corroborate Michael Jackson's innocence, but neither did the plaintiff who accused Michael Jackson of child molestation. The D.A.'s office did not need the testimony of the little boy if they could have found the smallest amount of credible evidence to corroborate the 13-year old boy's accusations.

I am merely painting a picture that requires you to link all the pieces of the puzzle together. In some instances, I am directing you to look for facts that were buried.... that only someone from the inside can tell you where to search. Only those that are really in search of the real truth will find it.

Because of my spiritual beliefs, there are a lot of spiritual references contained in this book. I believe you cannot explain what happened in this case without pointing a finger at the real *spiritual culprit* that launched these allegations. While, at the same time, I feel it is necessary to let the world know that Michael Jackson has had God Almighty, the Creator of this universe on his side from the very beginning of these false allegations. God gave Michael Jackson what he didn't give the little boy, a witness (referred to in chapter six as *A Ram In the Bush*) who can attest to his innocence.

I am confident that after reading this book you will have the complete facts surrounding this case. These facts are based on what I witnessed and what I had documented in my work calendar diary; all put in chronological order. I have included information about facts that never came to the public's attention. I believe that it is in the public's best interest to know the whole truth concerning this case.

If you are reading this book for malicious gossip or evil intentions, you may be extremely disappointed. It is my hope that *Redemption* will shed light on the truth concerning this case. Real justice demands the truth. Then, and only then, can the process of healing begin.

To get the clearest picture of what happened you have to follow the chain of events in the order in which they occurred before, during and after the child molestation allegations came to the public's attention. To most of us, the allegation against Michael Jackson was just a flash bulletin on the news.

I am not trying to change anyone's mind, nor alter anyone's opinions concerning this case. I am simply telling my version of what I witnessed and believe really happened in this case. I have no evidence to offer other than a calendar diary that I kept during my employment with Barry Rothman. However, I offer my word that the information I am offering is the whole truth according to my recollection, perception and understanding.

It is never too late for truth to prevail, especially if the unproven allegations still cast shadows of guilt over someone's character. Then, and only then, can real freedom and justice prevail.

1.1
About The Author

In the summer of 1993 I worked for Barry Rothman, the attorney who represented the father of the little boy that accused Michael Jackson of child molestation. I am a 23-year veteran litigation legal secretary with recent experience as a law office manager. I am currently fulfilling my ministry call as an urban missionary working with at-risk children in Watts, California.

This is, in fact, my first attempt at writing a book. One of the reasons I have decided to come forth and write this book is because I have been carrying the information that I am about to reveal inside me since 1993. I have made several attempts since the onset of the case to try to get this information out to the public, but all of my efforts were to no avail. My first attempt was to give this information to the investigators who were seeking evidence and information to try the case in court. After the initial investigators and lawyers were switched and the course of the case went in a different direction, none of the information that I provided made it into court.

In 1997, four years after the child molestation allegations first surfaced, I heard an editor speak at a convention where he was encouraging people to search their hearts and see if they had something that was book worthy inside them. After returning from the conference, I realized that writing a book might be the best forum to put this information forward. It would allow the public to weigh the information presented and draw their own conclusions.

— REDEMPTION —

Since I had never written a book, and did not know anything about writing or selling a book, I had to do a great deal of research on the subject. After that was done, I then began the task of writing the first draft. In order to assure accuracy I brushed up on the facts concerning this case and incorporated my firsthand knowledge and crafted it so that a reader could see the story unfold just as it was being played out behind the scenes in 1993.

On more than one occasion I considered bowing out of the project because of the emotional stress and anxiety the process was causing me... but I persevered, figuring that time would eventually heal all wounds. Something inside me was continually gnawing at me, forcing me to complete a task that might have been given to me as a part of my destiny.

As I have mentioned before, I personally do not know Michael Jackson and do not know anyone that knows him. I just want the world to know what I have known for years. No matter what the press may say about Michael Jackson, I can emphatically attest to his innocence in this case because I was there.

During the outbreak of the child molestation allegations every news media outlet, tabloid magazine and reporter from around the world was trying to get a statement from the Chandler camp. Not only did the Chandler camp avoid the news media like the plague, they also refrained from making a statement and/or stating their position in any way, either about the allegations of sexual abuse or the lesser reported custody battle over the 13-year old Chandler boy that was going on at the same time.

It wasn't until the 13-year old boy sought representation by the well-known child attorney, Gloria Allred, that someone came forth to defend the boy's position. Gloria Allred stated that, "I'm ready and willing to go forward with the trial." However, within a couple of days of making that statement, she withdrew from the case. Reason, unknown!

Michael Jackson, on the other hand, came forth on several occasions, personally and through his attorneys and investigator, to make his innocence known to the world and assure his millions of fans, nationally and internationally, that he would be found innocent of the horrific charges against him. As of this date, Michael Jackson has never been charged with child molestation stemming from the 1993 allegations.

There were a lot of things about Michael Jackson being reported on the news and in the tabloids that were simply not true and, likewise, there were a lot of factual events that went unreported that were crucial in this case. A lot of the false information that was reported worldwide caused millions of people to believe that Michael Jackson was guilty of the single allegation of child molestation. Since then, Michael Jackson has made a lot of adjustments in his life, in my opinion, trying to live down the negative publicity that he endured. To a person who does not care about their image or being a role model, public scrutiny is not that important. But to a man that has always cared about his image, life-style, and being a role model... false negative publicity is mentally, physically and emotionally damaging to an innocent man—I don't care how strong his public image is.

No one should have to down play and cater to negative publicity just to regain a sense of emotional stability in their life. Justice is supposed to give the real victims the opportunity for closure and healing.

It is time for the truth surrounding the Michael Jackson child molestation allegations to be told. It is time to set the record straight.

* * *

The first thing that raised my suspicion that something was wrong in Mr. Rothman's office was the incredible amount of secrecy he maintained from all his employees when it came to the Chandler case. Instead of the usual activities that happened during most cases, the Chandler case began to look more like scheming and plotting. My suspicion caused me to begin making notes of events in my monthly calendar book as they were taking place (referred to in Mary Fisher's article: *Was Michael Jackson Framed?* in Gentlemen's Quarterly, as *the diary*). I have no idea why I felt the need to take notes of events and statements because at that time I had no idea of what was on the horizon other than the outcome of the custody battle that was taking place. I was merely noting dates for my own recollection. I can, however, declare truthfully that my 1993 calendar book has not been written in since 1993.

All entries in my 1993 calendar book were written in chronological sequence and can stand the scrutiny of a forensic ink dating test. In other words, the calendar book that has been widely referred to has not been altered, and the entries were initially made for my own reference and to jar my own memory prior to my knowledge of the child molestation allegations being launched against Michael Jackson.

No one was privy to the information contained in this book except my immediate family and close friends who helped me live with the emotional anxiety that I encountered while working with Mr. Rothman during the onset of this case. My only outlet was confiding with my mother and close friends. My mother's assistance was instrumental in giving me the strength to contact the investigation team working for Michael Jackson when the news of the child molestation allegations surfaced.

Just the knowledge of typing letters and court documents that sparked the child molestation allegation was troublesome to me. Although suspicious, I had no idea that the case would turn out the way it did or that it was leading anywhere near what would come to pass. The only thing that was clear to me in spite of all the office secrecy was the child custody battle. The allegation of child abuse was being played out below the surface so as not to draw any attention, even to the in-house office staff.

Something that was, and still is, very puzzling to me was why did the public, experts and the media ignore obvious facts that pointed to Michael Jackson's innocence, (that I will address in detail later)? I realize that we live in a society that loves to see giants fall, especially if that giant is African-American and crossing long established barriers of color. I am not saying that race had anything to do with this case — greed is a demon all by itself. However, why were many facts pointing to his innocence brushed aside and the voice of one child allowed to completely crucify the character of a mega-star who had lived an impeccable life-style all his life?

Mega-stars of Michael Jackson's status traditionally have lived shady life-styles of drugs, alcohol, multi-marriages and divorces. Michael Jackson's life-style began to take on some of these characteristics only after enduring the pain and humiliation of the child molestation allegation. Somehow the hype behind the allegations caused people to forget who he really was and the life-style that he had demonstrated throughout his entire life. Why was it that the public suddenly forgot the Michael Jackson that supported thousands of charities throughout the years, helped many children achieve their goals of education, helped schools financially and supported many foundations? Why did the public forget that Michael Jackson had spent his entire adult life supporting and helping children, not hurting them?

The Bible says that, "you shall know a tree by the fruit that it bears." Why did we forget the Michael Jackson that we have known since his early entertainment years of blessing millions of people with his incredible talent and life? These are the deeds that go to the heart of who Michael Jackson is. His only acts toward children were to support them, give them love, nurture them, and show them kindness — giving them a sense of hope, pride, opportunity, love and attention. It is a shame that the very thing he loved the most was used as a weapon against him.

Unfortunately, humanitarian stories of people helping one another seldom make the headlines. We live in a society that loves to hear the bad news and feeds on vicious gossip. Hurt and pain dominate the news media and tabloid magazines. Even notorious criminals are elevated to the place of stardom. Although we live in a society where the justice system says that we are, "innocent until proven guilty," too much negative press desensitizes us into believing the worst until the innocence of a man or woman can be proven in court.

Michael Jackson was not found guilty in a court of law. He was found guilty through the media in the hearts and minds of millions of people throughout the world. The media was being fueled by reports from anyone having anything to say that seemed to corroborate the child molestation allegations. The media was willing to pay former employees of Michael Jackson thousands of dollars just for the mere accusation of wrongdoing by him.

The news media operates under a system of reporting information that will draw public attention, whether or not it's true, in order to increase sales or ratings. Although it's not the media's fault that stories about murders, rapes, wars, turmoil, scandal and child molestation, especially at the hands of a public figure, are a box office draw. It's simply the society that we live in. Some might call it the godless society, but nonetheless, reports about people helping one another, doing good deeds or positive news reporting do not draw the public's attention like a blood dripping sex scandal coated with marshmallows and smothered in cream. Producers and editors are under constant pressure to compete with other networks and newspapers. They are not trying to change society by reporting positive, wholesome, uplifting and humanitarian stories, but to boost ratings. There are, however, quality segments on all newscast programming that gives a spotlight for heroic and humanitarian reports—just all too rarely reported—they don't boost ratings.

* * *

In the following pages I will also address the extortion allegation made against Dr. Chandler and Mr. Rothman. It is my opinion that if the extortion allegation had been investigated as extensively and vigorously as the child molestation allegation, it may have answered a lot of unanswered questions. The police left no stone unturned while investigating the child molestation allegations made against Michael Jackson. They interrogated his past, present and then current employees and traveled out of the country to investigate former employees regarding their statements that they witnessed inappropriate behavior by Michael Jackson with young children. After thousands of dollars were spent trying to indict Michael Jackson, no credible evidence was found to corroborate the charge of child molestation against him.

Dozens of children were interviewed, even the friends of the children that knew Michael Jackson were interviewed. Still, no indictment of child molestation was made. It quickly became obvious that the same resources that went into trying to find evidence against Michael Jackson were not used to investigate the extortion allegations that would have cleared his name.

Michael Jackson has been the victim of unwanted public scrutiny without any evidence or proof for many years. When the child molestation allegations surfaced against him, the public seemed relieved to finally have something *credible* instead of giving him the benefit of the doubt, or even the benefit of his rights provided by the Constitution of the United States. The only justification that the media could find was that in their opinion, "it isn't normal for a 35-year old male adult to spend so much time with children or to sleep with them." That statement was mere speculation. It does not prove guilt nor invalidate his innocence. Our tainted untrusting world seems to have difficulty understanding pure and simple love. Michael Jackson repeatedly voiced his love, admiration and affection for the innocence of children, reliving a childhood that he himself missed out on. How many of us know men and women who are still living out their childhood well into their 40's, 50's and even 60's. Just going to an amusement park and getting on frightening roller-coasters is our way of reliving the fearless days of childhood. Why is it difficult for us to comprehend that a person who is restricted in his ability to mingle and interact with adult human beings in public on a daily basis, ever since his childhood, finds enjoyment in the pureness and innocence of a child's company?

This type of affection is especially common for someone who did not or does not have children of their own. People like this tend to adopt other people's children as their own. In Michael Jackson's case, he always had a child around him that he favored and who would ultimately become his traveling companion. At one time it used to be his monkey, at another time it was Brook Shields. Different companions — same loving Michael Jackson.

There is no doubt that the penal system is unfair to poor people who are unable to hire private attorneys to defend their case. In Michael Jackson's case, he had the best lawyers and investigators that money could buy, but you will not begin to understand an important piece of the puzzle as to why Michael Jackson settled the case until you read the chapter entitled, Legally Speaking. I went into great detail to help people that are not familiar with the United States Justice System to understand what was taking place in the court system that caused Michael Jackson's lawyers to advise him to settle the case rather than proceed with the case. There had to be a reason other than credible evidence. If they had obtained credible evidence of his guilt, Michael Jackson would have been indicted and tried criminally by the D.A.'s office.

In my opinion, the only thing worse than someone being crucified for a crime they did not commit, is being crucified for a crime they were not even charged with.

One reason I am coming forth with this book is to set the record straight. It is also my hope that *Redemption* will do just as it implies — redeem and bring closure, healing and repentance for all involved.

Several articles and books have been written expressing beliefs of Michael Jackson's innocence. Only someone from the inside can accurately explain the chain of events that led up to the child molestation allegations. Absent any physical evidence supporting the child molestation allegations, all angles of the case must be explored and given equal weight. I will examine simple truths that were staring us straight in the face all along. The true facts concerning this case are as simple as 1, 2, 3... A,B,C. All you, the reader, have to do is put the chain of events into chronological order. Let the information that was reported worldwide speak for itself. In other words, let's be honest with ourselves for a change. You be the judge.

To those who would say I am coming forth just to make money, would be underestimating my main purpose for writing this book. I could have come forth long before now if I was money-driven. To say that I am coming forth for notoriety purposes would be a typical assumption, but that too is not correct—considering that I dislike public attention. If someone were to say that it is time for the truth to be told, you have just started to scratch the surface of my motive. If you conclude that it is time for truth *and* justice—I'd say BINGO! You've just got to know the heart of the author of this book.

Part 2
The Main Characters

2.1
Rothman - The Lawyer

Barry Rothman was the attorney that represented Dr. Evan Chandler, the father of the 13-year old boy that accused Michael Jackson of child molestation. I came to work for him as an independent contractor — legal secretary during the summer of 1993. Mr. Rothman was a well-known entertainment attorney in Century City, California. He represented and negotiated music and concert deals for many very famous rock groups and even some legends of the music industry. The decor of Mr. Rothman's office was filled with gold and platinum records hanging on the walls. Mr. Rothman is very distinguished in his appearance, very well dressed and has salt-and-pepper hair. At the time I worked for him he drove a 1977 Rolls-Royce Corniche.

If, however, you walked behind the scenes of Mr. Rothman's office, you will find a different person altogether. According to an article written by Mary Fisher of GQ in 1994, "Rothman has a reputation for stiffing people." He was considered a professional deadbeat who pays no one. Professionally, he has received repeated disciplinary actions by the State Bar.

For security reasons his office is set up like Fort Knox. No one can just walk into his office and gain access to him from the outside. He always entered his office with extreme caution. During the Michael Jackson child molestation allegations, he would always call the office before arriving to see if anything unusual was going on before he arrived. It was as if he was checking in everyday to see if the coast was clear. Or, checking to see if anyone was waiting for his arrival.

The entrance to Mr. Rothman's office was set up so that it did not allow anyone to gain access without being buzzed in. The office had two front doors — one led into the lobby and the second led into the office. The door that led into the office was always locked. The reception area had a shutter that could only be opened by someone from the inside. An intercom allowed the receptionist to communicate with anyone entering the front lobby without them gaining access to the office. Once she identified them she would buzz them into the office. I always felt uncomfortable under such lock and key.

Once Mr. Rothman arrived at the office, his instant presence would ruin what was, up to that moment, a quiet atmosphere. His arrival would immediately create a disturbing and hostile atmosphere of yelling, disgust and anger. My best description of an encounter with Mr. Rothman is a real-life encounter with a real life demon straight out of the pits of hell. Although I have never met a real life demon straight out of the pits of hell, after encountering Mr. Rothman I knew what it would feel like.

When I started work in the summer of 1993 as an independent contractor for Mr. Rothman as his sole legal secretary, it was the beginning of a work relationship I will never forget. One like I had never encountered and never have since. His office consisted of one legal secretary, one receptionist and two other associate attorneys; one male and one female. Mr. Rothman had no respect for the attorneys that worked for him. I would often overhear him yelling at them like they were regular staff and badgering the female attorney like she was a child. I never saw him treat anyone with respect.

The receptionist was hired around the same time as I was. She was a beautiful redhead, soft spoken, shy and a very efficient young lady. Mr. Rothman demanded that she make his coffee every morning, pour his coffee and carry it into his office, and serve it to him on a serving tray. He treated her more like a waitress instead of a professional law office receptionist.

— REDEMPTION —

It's normal for the support staff to provide attorneys and clients with coffee and beverages, but it is unusual to find a law firm that requires the professional staff to make the attorney breakfast and lunch on a daily basis, as well as shopping for the food to be used for the attorney's personal consumption. Mr. Rothman required all of the above. He even required the receptionist to shop for his food on her own time before or after work. It was written all over her face that this was causing her a lot of humiliation and was demeaning to her professionally. She literally had to wait on him hand and foot and do tasks that were ordinarily not required of the staff in a professional law office.

Instead of being grateful for her willingness to provide him with ordinary services, Mr. Rothman treated her like a whipping post. She was under daily verbal attack by Mr. Rothman. He humiliated and yelled at her for the slightest mistake or misunderstanding. Usually, his instructions were unclear or not complete and he would yell at her as if he expected her to read his mind. He would often yell at the top of his lungs only a few inches from her face. She had to endure spit flying across her face, while afraid to say anything because he was irrational. Mr. Rothman's mannerism was often intimidating and physically threatening. When he was in the midst of a full-fledged tantrum it appeared as if he was going to physically attack you at any moment.

I never saw him smile at his employees. When he did smile he displayed a set of pearly white teeth that appeared to have cost him a great deal of money. The receptionist sat right outside Mr. Rothman's door; therefore, she was in his direct line of fire and was constantly in tears. It made her a nervous wreck.

To keep from responding emotionally to the things that were going on around me, I had to carry myself as a true professional. The attitude I had to develop, just to make it through the day was, that, "it was just a job." However, after witnessing the constant friction, yelling and emotional outbursts, I also felt emotionally drained at the end of every day. The only way I could live peacefully with Mr. Rothman was to bury my head in my work and pay close attention to my work quality. For me, it was fortunate that my work quality was exceptional and that often gave me favor with the savage beast. I did, however, have a few conflicts with Mr. Rothman. It was mainly over small, insignificant things. He would find one little error and storm all the way to the back of the office like a Trojan warrior, just to yell at me for an error in which you needed a magnifying glass to see. I would simply appease his tantrum and nod at the appropriate time to get him off my back. It required that you not argue with him at all. That would only serve in increasing his wrath. You could get rid of him quickly if you simply said nothing but, "yes... uh hum... I understand... okay, I'll correct it."

Working for Mr. Rothman, however, was a true test to even my own intestinal fortitude and philosophy. All of my perceived notions and remedies did not prepare me for dealing with Mr. Rothman's character. For the most part, Mr. Rothman would play it pretty cool with me because I was a good legal secretary and he had run the gambit of good secretarial support. He appreciated my work quality and my level of professionalism.

One year prior, Mr. Rothman was located on Sunset Boulevard. He apparently had so many secretaries that he did not remember that I had temped for him once before. Mr. Rothman told me upon starting that his prior secretary had just quit and stole a lot of office equipment from his office, such as a typewriter, dictaphone, fax machine, etc. On my first day of work he told me about the incident and I thought it was strange for a professional legal secretary to do such a thing. However, after working for Mr. Rothman and observing his employer tactics, I could understand why, even though I do not condone that type of behavior under any circumstances.

According to public records, Mr. Rothman filed bankruptcy in 1992 with debts totaling almost one million dollars. He moved from the Sunset Boulevard office owing Folb Management $53,000 in back rent, claiming that the building's security was inadequate and caused him a loss of $6,900 worth of office equipment from the secretarial burglary. The office equipment that he told me was stolen from his office did not add up to $6,900. This demonstrates Mr. Rothman's ethics in handling his financial responsibilities—as will be discussed later on, I witnessed this behavior from Mr. Rothman on several occasions.

Public records also indicate that Mr. Rothman's assets were owned by fictitious or holding corporations. This is a well-known corporate scheme that is designed to protect your assets if someone sues you. It requires that you open multiple corporations; one to act as a holding corporation (which owns all your assets) and one to act as a shell corporation (that sits dormant until needed to start a fresh corporation immediately after defuncting the existing corporation). When the operating corporation falls into trouble due to lawsuits, tax liens, etc., you take your shell corporation off the shelve, open up a bank account, and you are back in business the next day as a new corporation. Because the assets are owned by the holding corporation, this keeps the corporate assets from being levied against when someone sues the main corporation. The corporate entity that is holding the assets cannot be sued because it is specifically created to be a holding corporation and does not engage in business. Therefore, the corporate scheme is that when the main corporation is sued, it has no assets to be levied upon to pay the judgment. In reality, however, a sharp bankruptcy trustee can find assets wherever they are and expose corporate schemes.

Mr. Rothman is a clever businessman. He had all of his assets protected. Even the title of his Rolls-Royce was transferred to a fictitious company that he controlled six months prior to filing bankruptcy. His corporate paperwork listed bogus addresses for several of his corporations. Dr. Chandler admitted to hiring Mr. Rothman because of his unethical business dealings. He needed someone that did not mind bending and/or breaking the rules.

Another very interesting fact about Mr. Rothman, on a smaller note, is that he has a twin brother who is also an attorney. I was told that his brother is an identical twin. Strangely enough, I noticed that he did not receive any phone calls from his brother the entire time that I worked for him. It is difficult for me to imagine Mr. Rothman having a double.

Rarely did family or friends call for Mr. Rothman at the office. Occasionally, his housekeeper would call him concerning matters around the house. Most of his calls came from clients or creditors leaving threatening messages for him to call them. One creditor called and threatened to *"drop a dime"* on Mr. Rothman if he did not get paid. Needless to say, when Mr. Rothman arrived at the office that was one call he returned immediately!

I also recall Mr. Rothman being a cigarette smoker who did not obey building ordinances which prohibited smoking in a public building. He smoked wherever he pleased — in your face or at your desk. He kept an ashtray at everyone's desk so he could walk throughout the office and have access to an ashtray wherever he went in the office. He had a bad habit of sitting his cigarette in the ashtray at your desk, forgetting it and then walking away with it still burning. The smell of smoke really bothered me, but I knew it would be useless to ask Mr. Rothman not to smoke in the office or around me. He chewed me out once for making that request. I decided to bide my time and walk lightly until I could get out of his office.

Mr. Rothman ran his office like a concentration camp. His goal was always to inflict pain, humiliate and render you worthless so he could feel more superior. In his eyes, there were only two classes of people, boss and employees. Even his associate attorneys fell under the employee classification because he treated them no differently. He would rant and rave and humiliate them publicly just like the clerical staff. We were all equally abused.

My desk was located at the back of Mr. Rothman's office only a few feet away from the large conference room. Most of the meetings held during the Michael Jackson case were held in this conference room allowing me to see and hear a great deal.... meetings between Mr. Rothman and Dr. Chandler, meetings between Mr. Rothman and Mr. Pellicano (Michael Jackson's investigator), and meetings with Dr. Chandler, his ex-wife, her husband and Mr. Rothman. The boy and his father also spent an enormous amount of time in this conference room after the child molestation allegations surfaced.

In addition to the building security, there was an incredible amount of in-house secrecy, which gave the impression that something fishy was going on. Usually law office staff, especially the legal secretary, are privy to the cases being handled by the attorney(s). They are involved at least on a clerical level; in that they type the correspondence, memos, timesheets and are hands-on with the client file. I recall being hands-on with Mr. Rothman's other cases, but not for the Chandler case. When it came to Dr. Chandler, everything was strictly confidential and meetings were held behind closed doors. Most of Dr. Chandler's calls were taken behind closed doors. Even when Mr. Rothman was talking to his associate attorneys and a phone call came in from Dr. Chandler, Mr. Rothman would interrupt and walk all the way back to his office, close the door and take the call in private.

In spite of this security, I was able to gather some information concerning the case from typing a few pleadings and correspondence. There were no memos to file, no follow-up correspondence to memorialize the many telephone conversations. Only the associate attorneys were privy to what was going on and they were only told what Mr. Rothman wanted them to know. I did, however, gain favor with the female associate attorney and learned a lot about Mr. Rothman, his practice and even some inside details concerning the case. I hold that information as confidential because she was a practicing attorney under the code of confidentiality. She did, however, give me a better understanding of what was going on in the office and surrounding the case, especially when it became public knowledge.

Two weeks before the child molestation allegation surfaced, our receptionist suddenly quit. She said she couldn't take Rothman's abuse anymore. Her timing was unfortunate for

Mr. Rothman because when the child molestation allegations hit the media our phones rang off the wall constantly. During the time of her employment at Mr. Rothman's office she and I became very good friends. I was always comforting her when Mr. Rothman would drive her to tears. I talked her out of quitting a couple of times before, but I could tell that she was fed up!

She did not feel comfortable telling him of her plan to quit to his face because she did not trust him. She informed me of her plan to go to the bank after receiving her paycheck, cash it and then call Mr. Rothman on the phone and advise him that she quit. She wanted to make sure that her check was cashed and in the bank before he knew of her plans to quit. Her impromptu departure left us without a receptionist just before the Michael Jackson allegations surfaced. Mr. Rothman's efforts to replace the receptionist allowed me to see just how shrewd he really was.

In a six-week period we went through a series of replacement receptionists. Not because we couldn't find a good receptionist, but because we could not find a receptionist who could fit the demands of Mr. Rothman. Most of the receptionists did not last more than one or two days. The ones that lasted one to two weeks were exceptional. However, in their second week, Mr. Rothman would create a big ruckus over something small, or just simply needle them on every tiny issue, until he succeeded in causing them to walk off the job. Once the receptionist would walk off the job because of his harassment, Mr. Rothman would simply call the agency that he hired them from and complain of THEIR inadequacy and refuse to pay the bill. I watched Mr. Rothman pull this stunt on at least three occasions. By the third time the agency started getting wise to Mr. Rothman's scheme. This would cause him to change agencies and he would pull the same stunt on the new agency.

As for the receptionists, I watched one girl break down into tears just before walking off the job. Another receptionist was pretty strong hearted but after Mr. Rothman hammered her into the ground on minor issues; she went to lunch and had a few drinks before coming back to the office. Mr. Rothman complained to the agency that she was an alcoholic. She obviously needed a drink to continue working with Mr. Rothman. He attacked another lady on her first day of employment and left her shaking like a leaf. She was able to handle the pressure, but she called it quits around the second week.

Even switching to a different agency didn't work. The word between the agencies must have spread, causing them to request cash up-front before they would even send a candidate out to our office. It was highly unusual for an agency to require cash payment in advance—but absolutely necessary when dealing with Mr. Rothman.

Definition: *Sabotage* - "The act or process tending to hamper or hurt. Deliberate subversion."

Subversion - "A cause of overthrow or destruction."

Dr. Chandler described Mr. Rothman as "nasty, cruel and that he was going to destroy everybody in sight in any devious way." I witnessed Dr. Chandler's description of Mr. Rothman's behavior almost on a daily basis.

Most of the time attorneys are trustworthy and carry themselves, with staff and clients, on a professional basis. They are held to a high professional standard and code of ethics. If you are able to afford their legal fees, you will generally receive quality and professional services. I know there are individuals who may have had unfavorable experiences with attorneys or law firms. I can only speak for myself and what I have heard from others. I do not want anyone reading this book to think that all attorneys are like Mr. Rothman. Mr. Rothman is in a class all by himself. I also do not want to discourage anyone from hiring an attorney should they need one, or from working in the legal field or discourage anyone from becoming an attorney. What I experienced with Mr. Rothman, I have never experienced with any other attorney or law firm in my entire legal career.

The legal profession is, to me, one of the greatest fields in which to work. It is challenging and full of excitement, with all levels of professional people working side by side towards the same goal of winning and providing the client with the best care and representation. Law firms generally do an outstanding job for their clients. It is understandable that not every side can win and that someone must lose, but not every loss is a result of attorneys not doing a good job. The reasons why a judge or jury end up taking one side over the other is little understood. It can be due to numerous reasons, including what side of the bed the judge got up on the morning of the trial. In any case, at least the losing attorney or law firm can usually rest assured knowing they fought fair, and put up a good and fair fight for the sake of their client.

The duties and obligations of an attorney, as it relates to their clients, according to the State Bar of California are as follows:

a.) To support the Constitution and laws of the United States and of this state.

b.) To maintain the respect due to the courts of justice and judicial officers.

c.) To counsel or maintain such actions, proceedings, or defenses only as appear to him or her legal or just, except the defense of a person charged with a public offense.

d.) To employ, for the purpose of maintaining the causes confided to him or her such means only as are consistent with truth, and never to seek to mislead the judge or any judicial officer by an artifice or false statement of fact or law.

e.) To maintain inviolate the confidence, and at every peril to himself or herself to preserve the secrets, of his or her client.

f.) To abstain from all offensive personality, and to advance no fact prejudicial to the honor or reputation of a party or witness, unless required by the justice of the cause with which he or she is charged.

g.) Not to encourage either the commencement or the continuance of an action or proceeding from any corrupt motive of passion or interest.

h.) Never to reject, for any consideration personal to himself or herself, the cause of the defenseless or the oppressed.

I.) To cooperate and participate in any disciplinary investigation or other regulatory or disciplinary proceeding pending against the attorney. However, this subdivision shall not be construed to deprive an attorney of any constitutional or statutory privileges.

j.) To comply with the requirements of Section 6002.1.

k.) To comply with all conditions attached to any disciplinary probation, including a probation imposed with the concurrence of the attorney.

l.) To keep all agreements made in lieu of disciplinary prosecution with the agency charged with attorney discipline.

m.) To respond promptly to reasonable status inquiries of clients and to keep clients reasonably informed of significant developments in matters with regard to which the attorney has agreed to provide legal services.

n.) To provide copies to the client of certain documents under time limits and as prescribed in a rule of professional conduct which the board shall adopt.

o.) To report to the agency charged with attorney discipline, in writing, within 30 days of the time the attorney has knowledge of any of the following: [omitted]

Rules of Professional Conduct

Where attorneys exercise undue influence over clients or take unfair advantage of clients, discipline is appropriate. (See, e.g., Magee v. State Bar (1962) 58 Cal.2d 423 [24 Cal.Rptr. 839]; Lantz v. State Bar (1931) 212 Cal. 213 [298 P. 497].)

2.2
The 13-Year old Boy

Michael Jackson first met the 13-year old Chandler boy, that would later make the allegations against him, at a Rent-A-Wreck car rental agency. The agency was owned by Dave Schwartz, the husband of June Chandler (June Schwartz) who is the mother of the boy who accused Michael Jackson of child sexual abuse. When Michael Jackson's car broke down, Dave Schwartz found out that he was coming to his agency to rent a car. He called June Schwartz and told her to bring their 13-year old son, who was a fan of Michael Jackson, to the office. Michael Jackson felt a sense of devotion towards the boy after being told that he sent him a picture that he drew after his hair caught on fire during filming of a commercial.

From the moment Michael Jackson met the boy they became friends. Michael Jackson began calling the boy and lavishing him and his mother with expensive gifts, shopping sprees and trips all over the world; including Monaco and Paris.

I had the opportunity to meet the 13-year old boy on two separate occasions while working with Mr. Rothman. The first meeting was unexpected. I stumbled upon the 13-year old boy by surprise in Mr. Rothman's office behind closed doors as I was preparing to leave work. It was required that we check in with Mr. Rothman before leaving to see if he needed anything before we left the office. Mr. Rothman was in his office with the doors closed, and that generally meant you had to knock first. Without thinking, I opened his office door to say goodbye,

— REDEMPTION —

and to my surprise, I saw a young boy around 12 to 13 years old at the back of Mr. Rothman's office. I knew he was the Chandler boy because that was the only case, to my knowledge, that Mr. Rothman was working on which involved a child. I was, however, very surprised to see the boy in Mr. Rothman's office unaccompanied by a parent. The boy, likewise, was surprised when I opened the door. Mr. Rothman snapped at me for entering unannounced. I had not even seen the boy enter Mr. Rothman's office, nor did Mr. Rothman announce that he was meeting with a child. It appeared as if the meeting between Mr. Rothman and the boy was a secret. I glanced at the boy for a second and pretended as though everything was normal before leaving the office. The boy had a puzzled look on his face when I walked into Mr. Rothman's office. That made me very suspicious of this meeting between Mr. Rothman and the Chandler boy. I had the most overwhelming feeling that this meeting had some significance to the child molestation allegations and not the custody case that was also going on between the boy's parents. This meeting between Mr. Rothman and the Chandler boy took place just before the boy was taken to see the psychiatrist who later reported the sexual molestation charges against Michael Jackson.

The second time I met the 13-year old boy was after the child molestation allegations hit the media. Dr. Chandler and his son came to our office to hide from the media frenzy that erupted immediately thereafter. No one was prepared for the public's response to the allegations. Dr. Chandler was afraid to go home because his yard was crawling with news media and the media was desperately trying to find Dr. Chandler and his son, who were both hiding in our office. Mr. Rothman demanded that I work overtime that evening to type some legal documents for them.

While Mr. Rothman and Dr. Chandler were secretly hashing out details of their next move in the conference room, the boy kept walking back and forth between the conference room and my desk. I remember that he was amazed at my ability to type over 100 words per minute. He asked me, "how can you type so fast?" He kept staring at my keyboard with amazement. Once, while he was near my desk, I asked him how he was doing. He stated that he was doing fine.

While he was observing me, I too, was observing him. He was playing with some toys while listening to a Walkman radio. He seemed to be enjoying himself. I am not sure if he knew exactly what was going on outside of Mr. Rothman's office, but at least for the moment he seemed to be having a good time. From all appearances he seemed like a perfectly normal child interested in playing and listening to his music and was curious about everything.

I observed the boy going in and out of the conference room where his father was nervously going round and round with Mr. Rothman. The father was far more nervous than his son. The boy seemed to just stay in his own imaginary world playing, having fun and not seemingly worried about what was going on with the outside world.

I understood why Michael Jackson was fond of the boy. He was very fun, loving, warm spirited and cute. I found myself drawn to his warm and loving personality. He was not your normal bratty kid — he was very kind and had a gentle personality. He did not act or appear as though he had been harmed in any way. He was acting like any normal, well behaved 13-year old child.

Although I do not have enough psychological experience to know how a child would act who had been sexually abused, I can say that there was nothing abnormal about his behavior, personality or attitude. In fact, he was the one who kept calming and consoling his father, who was a nervous wreck. It appeared as if the boy was protecting his father instead of vice-versa. He was more concerned about his father's well-being than his own.

After observing the boy for a number of hours, I could not help but speculate, in my mind, *what would cause a child to falsely accuse someone of child abuse*? Especially someone he loved and valued as a good friend — especially someone like Michael Jackson! Most kids would give their right arm and leg to be close to the superstar. I could not stop wondering how this boy could be sucked into such a scheme as this. What could make such an innocent child become part of such an evil scheme?

It was obvious to me the boy felt a sense of duty towards his father. He kept walking back and forth checking on his father and asking if he was alright. When the father would have a nervous outburst the boy would soothe him and calm him down. The situation between the boy and his father reminded me of when I used to work for a juvenile attorney and handled many cases of child abuse. It was always procedure for the social worker to ask the child(ren), after removing them from the abusive environment, if they wanted to return to live with the parent. In at least 95% of all cases the child said "yes". In most cases, the child would cover up and try to protect the parent, knowing that the parent was wrong or had lied.

I know from firsthand experience how a manipulating parent can and will use his/her child(ren), and encourage them to participate or help execute a devious scheme. The parent often entices and lures the child's co-participation by promising them something of great value, especially in cases where there is a divorce or separation. Both parents try to gain the greatest influence over the other by offering the child bigger or better prizes. It almost appears as though they are fighting for the child's affection. But only a parent, or someone of great influence, can make a child override their sense of right and wrong. After all, isn't it the parents who teach the child their moral values?

Another technique I've seen used by parents to gain influence over their children is to place a *guilt trip* on the child by telling them how much this will help them if the child cooperates and goes along with the plan. How they will be able to do this... or that...if the child plays along. Children can be quite imaginative with the proper coaching and instructions.

Only a child could have caused Michael Jackson to let his guard down. It appears that Michael Jackson's only error was that he trusted in the innocence of a child. Since missing out on so much of his own childhood and being trapped in a world of seclusion, he could easily identify with a child because of his childlike personality. I imagine that, to him, being around children was like reliving his childhood, one that he was robbed of while pursuing stardom.

For Michael Jackson the kiss of death, a modern day Judas, came in the form of a child. A child was apparently used to bring Michael Jackson down, while being coached and manipulated by adults. The same child upon whom he had lavished gifts, trips and tours. Just a couple of months before the child abuse allegations surfaced, the boy, his mom and stepsister accompanied Michael Jackson to an award show in Morocco. Prior to the custody battle between the boy's parents, Michael Jackson offered to take the boy, his mom and sister on the *Dangerous World Tour*. It was this proposed excursion that sparked the custody battle.

A child, however, could not have done this alone. It is interesting to note that prior to the child abuse allegations, the boy's father was trying to raise money to produce his own movie. The boy shared that same interest with his father. Just months before, in July 1993, the boy's father co-wrote the movie, *Robin Hood: Men in Tights,* with Mel Brooks and David Shapiro. It is my understanding that the idea for the movie came from the boy and his father co-wrote it with the other writers. The movie was a success and played in theaters worldwide.

The idea to write *Robin Hood* came from the 13-year old Chandler boy long before he met Michael Jackson. Out of all the news reports that I heard concerning this case, the fact that the boy and his father had an interest in producing movies was down-played or ignored. To be able to write movies, you must have a vivid imagination capable of creating believable story lines. The boy and his father demonstrated that they were creative enough to put their heads together and collaborate. Could the child molestation allegation have been another one of their brilliant works of collaboration?

2.3
Dr. Chandler - The Father of The 13-year old Boy

Dr. Chandler, the father of the boy who accused Michael Jackson of child abuse, was a dentist by trade; although he had hopes and aspirations of becoming a screenplay writer.

Dr. Chandler was born in the Bronx in 1944. Later in his life he moved to Los Angeles with his then wife, June Chandler. Dr. Chandler's marriage to June ended in divorce in 1985, and sole custody of their son was awarded to June Chandler.

Dr. Chandler's earlier dental profession started going downhill as a result of numerous lawsuits filed against his dental practice. He then moved and set up his practice in Beverly Hills and was successfully operating that practice at the time of the child molestation allegations.

Dr. Chandler continued to pursue his dream of becoming a successful screenplay writer, and as I mentioned earlier, co-wrote the Mel Brooks film, *Robin Hood: Men In Tights*. He experienced some degree of success with this movie and had a desire to have more of a controlling interest in another such project. In order to do this he needed a substantial amount of money.

Initially Dr. Chandler welcomed his son's friendship with Michael Jackson, even allowing Michael Jackson to stay at his house with his son. But all that began to change as the 13-year old boy and his family grew closer to Michael Jackson. It was speculated that Dr. Chandler became increasingly jealous over his son's affection toward the superstar, especially as the young boy began missing scheduled weekend visitations with his father.

It was also speculated that Dr. Chandler missed spending a lot of time with his son because of his own busy schedule. When Dr. Chandler realized that Michael Jackson was stealing his son's affection, he became furious with their friendship. I recall Dr. Chandler becoming extremely upset with his ex-wife for even considering to allow their son to travel with Michael Jackson on his upcoming *Dangerous Tour*. This meant that the boy would have to be taken out of school and a tutor hired in order for him to be able to travel with the superstar. This reportedly made Dr. Chandler irate. This was the beginning of the chain of events that sparked Dr. Chandler's anger towards Michael Jackson and started the child molestation allegation clock ticking.

In a secretly recorded telephone conversation between Dave Schwartz, the 13-year old boy's step father, and Dr. Chandler; Dr. Chandler admitted that he had been advised on what to say: and also admitted that he had paid people to move against Michael Jackson. In addition, he stated that everything was going according to a *plan*. The details of this conversation were not falsely trumped up. This was an actual tape recording between Dr. Chandler and Dave Schwartz, in which Dr. Chandler admitted he had a *plan* to destroy Michael Jackson if he didn't get what he wanted. What did he want? His relationship back with his son? To ruin the relationship between Michael Jackson and his son? No! Dr. Chandler had specifically stated his motive at this time was jealousy because he perceived that Michael Jackson was stealing his son's affection away from him. Dr. Chandler was angry, had a motive and saw an opportunity to make money.

Dr. Chandler did not, however, let his jealousy towards Michael Jackson stand in the way of asking him to build an addition to his house, supposedly so he could have more room while visiting his son. Michael Jackson briefly entertained the idea, but when he found out that his acquisition would not be approved by the building inspectors, Dr. Chandler then suggested that Michael Jackson simply buy him a new house. Dr. Chandler was already trying to capitalize on his son's friendship with Michael Jackson. It appears his mind was already calculating a way of reaping some type of profit from his son's friendship with Michael Jackson.

Dr. Chandler admitted, in his own words, that he had been "rehearsed about what to say," — "paid people to move against Michael" and that, "there was a *plan*." This was, in my opinion, a confession of guilt. Why wasn't anything done about this admission by Dr. Chandler? This tape recording of the actual conversation was played throughout the world. Everyone heard Dr. Chandler detailing his plot to destroy Michael Jackson if he "didn't get what he wanted."

Dr. Chandler further stated, "It's going to be bigger than all of us put together. The whole thing is going to crash down on everybody and destroy everybody in sight. It will be a massacre if I don't get what I want."

Dr. Chandler further went on to advise Dave Schwartz, in that same recorded telephone conversation, that he had hired an attorney named Barry Rothman because he is "DEVIOUS, NASTY and CRUEL, and will destroy everyone in sight." He also expressed that once his *plan* went forward he would "win big-time." I am not an attorney at law, but in laymen's terms, this sounds like he had expressed first degree, premeditated motives to extort money from Michael Jackson, all in one sentence — admittedly out of his own mouth and played on national and international television across the world.

Dave Schwartz asked Dr. Chandler, on numerous occasions, to consider the possible negative repercussions the case could have on his son. Dr. Chandler responded "…that's irrelevant to me." By Dr. Chandler's own admission, his actions had nothing to do with the best interest of his own child.

* * *

At this point I feel I need to mention that if Dr. Chandler really believed his son was sexually molested, why didn't he go to the police like most parents would in this situation? It is human instinct to want to see a perpetrator brought to justice for their crime. When the crime involves a child, the intensity for wanting justice, not money, is even higher. Although our legal system allows us to seek both justice and money, in this case Dr. Chandler only went after the money. Instead of filing criminal charges against Michael Jackson, Dr. Chandler commenced negotiating terms for a twenty million dollar movie deal.

Dr. Chandler appeared to be a very insecure man who was dominated by greed. The Bible says that "the love of money is the root of all evil." Dr. Chandler was the epitome of what the love of money can do to an individual. How the lust of money can turn an individual into a green-eyed monster with no regard for anyone — including their own child. Perhaps in some people's mind money can solve all problems. If that were so, why is it that so many people with wealth still have no peace or joy in their life? Money does nothing more than give the bearer access to natural resources and services, but it cannot buy peace or joy. Peace and joy only come from God and cannot be bought, rather it is given.

Dr. Chandler was clear about his intentions from the beginning. He stated in his conversation with Dave Schwartz, "I found the nastiest son-of-a-bitch I could find..." and "all he wants to do is humiliate as many people as he can." He was, of course, talking about my former employer, Barry Rothman. Dr. Chandler admitted that these are Mr. Rothman's key character traits.

2.4
David and June Schwartz - The Mother and Step-Father of the 13-year old Boy

June Schwartz, at times referred to as June Chandler, is the mother of the 13-year old boy who accused Michael Jackson of sexual misconduct. Her then husband, David Schwartz, owned the Rent-A-Wreck facility where Michael Jackson and the 13-year old boy first met.

Dave Schwartz played a strategic role in recording a conversation with Dr. Chandler, which was played throughout the world and gave a better understanding as to Dr. Chandler's motive for launching the false allegations. Dr. Chandler later filed a lawsuit against June and David Schwartz, alleging invasion of privacy and other charges as a result of the secretly recorded conversation.

In his complaint, Dr. Chandler accused David Schwartz of recording his conversation and giving it to a third party. David Schwartz, on the other hand, contends that he recorded his conversation with Dr. Chandler because of previous threats made by Dr. Chandler to kill his entire family, including the children. During the case I was often confused about the apparent on and off battles between Dr. Chandler and June and David Schwartz, because when the child molestation allegations surfaced they were all meeting together behind closed doors. The relationship between them at that point seemed normal and cordial.

June Schwartz later accused Dr. Chandler of conducting a cruel plan to gain control of the minor's assets. She further asserted that the action filed by Dr. Chandler was being brought to promote his own hope for celebrity status.

With all the time that Michael Jackson spent with the 13-year old boy in June Schwartz's presence, she stated that she never witnessed any inappropriate behavior by Michael Jackson.

David Schwartz cross-complained against Dr. Chandler for invasion of privacy. According to his Statement of Facts, he stated that he did not think Michael Jackson molested the 13-year old boy. He did, however, feel that his family was torn apart by Michael Jackson's interference.

Mr. Schwartz also spoke to the issue of Dr. Chandler's behavior as abusive, belligerent and violent. He stated that it was out of fear that he recorded the conversation. David Schwartz stated in his lawsuit against Dr. Chandler that he had been physically attacked on two occasions by Dr. Chandler. One attack was powerful enough to cause Dave Schwartz to lose consciousness.

June Schwartz acknowledged in her declaration, in support of her husband, that after the allegations of sexual abuse were made to the Department of Children's Services; they did interview the 13-year old boy in their home.

2.5
Pellicano - The Investigator

Anthony Pellicano was the private investigator brought into the case by Michael Jackson's long time attorney, Bertram Fields. He is well-known throughout the world as one of the best investigators available to the stars. His specialty is forensic wire tapping.

Anthony Pellicano single-handedly dug up all the pertinent facts surrounding this case. Once his investigation efforts were complete, there was no doubt in his mind that Michael Jackson was a victim of an elaborate extortion scheme at the hands of Dr. Chandler and Mr. Rothman. *Elaborate:* complex, intricate, detailed, sophisticated, highly structured.

It was Anthony Pellicano's efforts that produced the tape-recorded conversation between Dr. Chandler and Mr. Schwartz.

Immediately after Mr. Pellicano was brought into the case, his first course of action was to visit the boy at Michael Jackson's Century City condo where he and his sister were visiting. He asked the boy specific questions about whether Michael Jackson had done anything inappropriate. The boy repeatedly denied any wrongdoings by Michael Jackson. Mr. Pellicano reported that the little boy denied ever having sexual contact of any sort with Michael Jackson. This interview that Mr. Pellicano had with the little boy was consistent with the other interviews that were conducted with the many children who also had a close friendship with Michael Jackson over the years. Mr. Pellicano was careful to conduct the interview using the same protocols that social workers for the Department of Children's Services would have used. The interview was conducted in private and done without any parental influence whatsoever.

It wasn't until Mr. Pellicano was convinced of Michael Jackson's innocence that he began an aggressive all-out investigation by interviewing numerous witnesses who could corroborate Michael Jackson's innocence, as well as discrediting those who had claimed to witness inappropriate behavior by Michael Jackson.

Midway into the child molestation investigation, many bloodthirsty witnesses came forth providing the tabloids with statements of improper behavior by Michael Jackson towards the numerous children who had visited his Neverland Ranch. Mr. Pellicano's diligence and sophisticated investigative techniques significantly reduced the number of unreliable witnesses claiming to have damaging information against Michael Jackson.

I recalled typing letters to Mr. Pellicano, particularly the letter rejecting Michael Jackson's $350,000 counter-movie deal offer made to Dr. Chandler.

The first time I saw Mr. Pellicano was when he came to our office to try to get Mr. Rothman to discuss Michael Jackson's counter-movie deal offer of $350,000. The meeting took place behind closed doors. Mr. Pellicano stormed out of Mr. Rothman's office saying "shoot your best shot" and "that's extortion." To me he appeared to be furious with Mr. Rothman. It was apparent that they did not reach an agreement during that meeting. It is worth noting that Mr. Pellicano has a reputation of being a Sicilian hardball player and accustomed to dealing with oppositional individuals.

Mr. Pellicano stated from the beginning of the child molestation allegations that this case was only about money. After hearing a conversation taped by Mr. Schwartz, Mr. Pellicano must have felt even more certain the case was about extortion.

Just as Dr. Chandler had begun to carry out his threats to destroy Michael Jackson if he didn't get what he wanted, Mr.

— REDEMPTION —

Pellicano, likewise, began to step up his plans for a counter attack. Mr. Pellicano left no stone unturned in his pursuit of the truth. He vigorously pursued and interrogated witnesses for the defense attorneys. He would conduct an in-depth investigation of the witness prior to meeting with that individual. By the time he interviewed a witness he already had inside information regarding the extent of their involvement with the case.

My first face-to-face meeting with Mr. Pellicano was during an investigation meeting that was originally scheduled by my mother. She was the main reason I became involved in the investigation from the very beginning. She was privy to everything that I was encountering in this case. Because of her strong conviction to "not let anyone walk all over you," she could not sit by and do nothing with the information she was receiving. She found out who was investigating the case by keeping her eyes glued to all the TV news reports. That's how she found out Mr. Pellicano was the main private investigator for Michael Jackson and contacted him. Although my mother has since passed away, until her dying day she constantly reminded me to make sure I got the book out because she, too, realized that justice had not been served. At one point, after completing the book, I was extremely busy in the mission field and she begged me to give the book to her so she could find a publisher for the sake of getting it out. Because of the work that I was doing at the time, I felt the timing wasn't right for the release of the book. After all the smoke cleared and the pain subsided from losing a precious mother, her words served as a constant reminder to me, "don't forget to get the book out."

My mother contacted Mr. Pellicano and advised him to talk to me concerning the case because she felt I could help their investigation. At first, when my mother told me of the scheduled meeting, I thought I was meeting with the investigators from the District Attorney's office who were investigating the extortion allegations. I didn't know that private investigators were separate from the D.A.'s office. It wasn't until my meeting with Mr. Pellicano that I found out that he was a private investigator working for Michael Jackson.

Mr. Pellicano is a very tall, slender-built man, handsome and very gracious. He was a respectable man and had high regards for my mother's courage in persuading me to come forth. His office was immaculate, stylishly designed and had state-of-the-art computer equipment.

Convinced of Michael Jackson's innocence, Mr. Pellicano worked around the clock, collecting evidence to be used at the trial which was scheduled for March 21, 1994. It was Mr. Pellicano that produced a tape recorded conversation between Dr. Chandler and Mr. Schwartz in which Dr. Chandler admitted he was getting ready to execute a master plan which was going to destroy Michael Jackson if he didn't get what he wanted. The media played the tape recorded conversation all over the world. Even with this critical piece of evidence in Dr. Chandler's own voice, the police did not take the extortion charges seriously. Even in the face of this, Mr. Pellicano continued to compile evidence to aid in Michael Jackson's defense.

Mr. Pellicano also recorded a conversation with Mr. Rothman, Dr. Chandler's attorney, in which he tried to get Mr. Rothman to admit that Dr. Chandler only wanted money. Mr. Rothman, most likely being suspicious, didn't take Mr. Pellicano's bait. Mr. Pellicano and Mr. Rothman did, however, talk about the $350,000 counteroffer for one movie deal. Dr. Chandler refused the counteroffer because it wasn't enough for him to shut down his dental practice and work full-time on writing screenplays. It is my understanding that Dr. Chandler asked Michael Jackson for a film project of five million dollars per year for four years which totaled twenty million dollars, or he would go public with the child molestations allegations.

In the conversation between Mr. Pellicano and Mr. Rothman, he was successful in getting Mr. Rothman to openly discuss and negotiate the amount of money Dr. Chandler wanted to keep quiet about the allegations. The dictionary's definition of *extortion* is: "to obtain from a person by force or undue or illegal power." Also, "the act or practice of extorting money or other property." It was obvious from Dr. Chandler's and Mr. Rothman's own mouth, that they were negotiating the dollar amount required to keep quiet about the child molestation allegations. These conversations took place before the civil suit was filed and before the minor was taken to the psychiatrist who reported the child molestations allegation to the authorities.

At a press conference on August 24, 1993, Pellicano stated that the allegations of child molestation were the result of a failed twenty million dollar extortion attempt. He specifically stated that because Michael Jackson refused to pay the twenty million dollars, his refusal resulted in the child molestation allegations being launched.

I documented the last meeting between Mr. Pellicano and Mr. Rothman in my diary, which took place in Mr. Rothman's office on Friday, August 13, 1993. Mr. Pellicano stormed out of the office saying, "no way." That following Tuesday, August 17, 1993, Dr. Chandler took his son to see the psychiatrist who reported the child molestation allegations to the authorities.

What if Michael Jackson had agreed to pay the twenty million dollars? Would Dr. Chandler not have taken his boy to the psychiatrist? Could the visit to the psychiatrist in some way be a part of their plan? Make a mental note about this point which will be discussed in detail later on.

* * *

When Michael Jackson's attorney, Bert Fields brought in another attorney, Howard Weitzman, the defense took a different course. Mr. Fields and Mr. Pellicano vowed to fight the case to the bitter end. However, Mr. Weitzman was in favor of a settlement. They were constantly at odds with each other over the issue and it was even rumored that each was trying to take the lead role in representing Michael Jackson's multi million dollar career.

The difference in attorney strategy was that Michael Jackson's attorney, Mr. Fields, with the help of his investigator Mr. Pellicano, wanted to portray Michael Jackson as the victim of extortion. Mr. Weitzman, on the other hand, wanted to portray Michael Jackson as someone falsely accused of the charges, yet ready, willing and able to stand up to the public and assert his innocence. It was about that time that Michael Jackson returned to the United States and hosted several press conferences and conducted a rare talk show interview to set the record straight.

The extortion investigation lasted for approximately five months before it was dismissed immediately after the civil case was settled. (The dismissal of the extortion investigation may have been a provision of the settlement.) The highlights of the extortion case were the sophisticated investigation work done by Mr. Pellicano's office. It was Mr. Pellicano's office that secured the audio taped conversation between Mr. Schwartz and Dr. Chandler and later the recorded conversation between Mr. Pellicano and Mr. Rothman.

Mr. Pellicano also interviewed numerous child witnesses that were close to Michael Jackson and who had spent time at his ranch. They included children that had also spent the night at sleep-overs and had also shared Michael Jackson's bed. None of whom reported any wrongdoing by Michael Jackson — only good clean fun, which included pillow fights, food fights, pajama parties, and other childlike games.

Mr. Pellicano was later criticized for his efforts and accused of, "trying the case in the media." He was later plagued with motions to compel all the details of his investigation and to produce documents by Mr. Feldman's office. When Mr. Pellicano's attorneys tried to claim client privilege, Feldman quoted City of L.A. v. Superior Court, 170 Cal.App.3d 744, as his basis to deny his claim of privilege and admonished Pellicano about the risks involved in trying the case in the media.

Soon after this, it was announced in the media that Mr. Fields and Mr. Pellicano were no longer involved in the case.

From the reports in the media, Mr. Fields resigned following an incident in which he announced to the Court that, "an indictment would be upcoming." He later explained that his statement was, admittedly made in error, but only to delay the civil suit that was about to be filed by the 13-year old boy's attorney, Larry Feldman. Ordinarily, a civil suit is not filed until after the criminal case is completed. However, in this high profile case, nothing conformed to standard procedures.

I telephoned Mr. Pellicano and asked why he left the case. He told me he did not agree with the direction in which Mr. Weitzman was taking the case. He vehemently disagreed with the idea of settling with Dr. Chandler. He was angry at the thought of settlement and was fully convinced that if Michael Jackson would fight this out in court he would be exonerated. He further stated that he would have nothing to do with the settlement of this case. It was obvious that Mr. Pellicano was extremely angry and somewhat dismayed at the new direction in which the case was heading. He was genuinely upset that Dr. Chandler might get away with these charges and not be held responsible for his actions. Mr. Pellicano blatantly refused to pay what many felt was an extortion demand.

Mr. Pellicano never backed down from his opinion that this case was about extortion. He stated for the record in court documents that, "I have made statements to the effect that Dr. Evan Chandler and Barry Rothman are extortionists, because in my opinion that is exactly what they are."

2.6
Dr. Mantis Abrams - The Psychiatrist

Dr. Mantis Abrams is the mental health professional who reported the sexual abuse allegations against Michael Jackson to the proper authorities. He is also the doctor who Mr. Rothman sought out for an expert opinion to help establish the allegations against Michael Jackson. Mr. Rothman called Dr. Abrams and presented him with a hypothetical incident, apparently in order to gather information to aid him with his and Dr. Chandler's *plan*. On July 15th, Abrams sent Mr. Rothman a two-page letter stating that, "reasonable suspicion exists that sexual abuse may have occurred." Dr. Abrams further advised Mr. Rothman that if this were a real case, and not a hypothetical case, he would be required to report the matter.

Dr. Chandler used the letter that Dr. Abrams wrote to Mr. Rothman as a bargaining tool to start the negotiations for the twenty million dollar demand. Another medical expert advised that in order for a doctor to properly make a report of child abuse, he/she would have to interview the child making the claim. This letter was written entirely on Mr. Rothman's query without any contact with the child in question.

It was Dr. Abrams' report to the Department of Children's Services that sparked the investigation against Michael Jackson. The Department of Children's Services was obligated to make a report of this type to the police department, and in doing so, search warrants were issued to search Michael Jackson's residences.

Dr. Abrams was required by law to report any evidence of child abuse. As embarrassing as it might be to the accused individual, every incident of child abuse and/or molestation must be investigated. There are too many real cases of child abuse and molestation that go unreported and undetected. Some cases are not reported until the child reaches adulthood and only discovered after the individual enters counseling. Needless to say, founded acts, such as this, bring about emotional scars that the victims carry for life.

I find no fault in Dr. Abrams' position and actions in this case. I believe he was being used as a pawn to bring credibility without question to the allegation of child molestation against Michael Jackson.

Thank God for professionals doing their job.

2.7
Michael Jackson - The Icon

Musically, Michael Jackson is known as the King of Pop. His music career speaks for itself. His record sales have surpassed the sales of legends of the past, such as Elvis Presley and the Beatles, just to name a few. He is not known throughout the world as the greatest black entertainer, simply the greatest. Michael Jackson's fans—young, old, rich, poor, white and black all know him as the greatest entertainer ever.

Michael Jackson has lived an impeccable life-style since rising to fame as a child star, unlike other stars who have lived lives who have been less than perfect—Michael Jackson has but one vice: bringing happiness to the world, especially to children. His comments to the allegation of molesting the boy was, "I would never hurt a child."

Apparently his accusers were ignorant of the facts regarding Michael Jackson, the humanitarian. Michael Jackson raised over one hundred million dollars through his *Dangerous World Tour* and donated all the proceeds to his Heal the World Foundation. He donates many more millions of dollars, as well as his time, visiting children in hospitals all around the world.

Michael Jackson has been a role model to millions of adoring fans. His fans have a deep love for him and view him as their hero. One who uplifts them through his music, and encourages world peace and love. His song *Man In The Mirror* encourages people to make a change by starting with the man in the mirror. His song *We Are the World* was a best selling single and he donated the proceeds to the USA for Africa charity. Michael Jackson uses his influence and money to help a hurting world. He does not fit the normal profile of someone who would molest a child. Just the opposite. He has spent his life helping innocent children.

Michael Jackson has lived a spotless life until these allegations were levied against him. From the moment they were made, he was under constant media bashing and the subject of unfounded rumors by the media trying to portray him as a sinister evil child molester. The media did, in fact, assassinate Michael Jackson's character through the child molestation allegations by constantly reporting unsubstantiated rumors, whether true or not, and withholding news that would have leaned in the singer's favor. For instance, they did not report that the TWO grand juries, one in Santa Barbara and the other in Los Angeles, could not find a single credible piece of evidence to indict Michael Jackson of the child molestation charges. Network and cable TV producers did not interrupt their normal programming to advise the world that, NO EVIDENCE COULD BE FOUND TO INDICT MICHAEL JACKSON OF CHILD MOLESTATION, countering their initial reports and accusations. The media, instead, let that news go unreported and/or did not place the same significance about bringing the information to light as they had to the more salacious accusations, and they allowed all the allegations of child molestation to be reported. The earlier reports were allowed to remain embedded in the minds of millions of Americans and others throughout the world.

Many say that Michael Jackson is like a child trapped in a man's body. His Neverland Ranch is similar to a fairy-tale land which he opens up to hundreds of children each year. Others say he is living out the childhood that he missed by entering the entertainment industry at an early age. It is my contention that because of his megastar multimillion dollar status, who could Michael Jackson trust? Children are known for their innocence and untarnished love. I believe he feels comfortable around children because all they want to do is play games and have fun. They don't place a price tag on their friendship nor a demand for love. In a child's heart, if they like you, you are just another person no matter your social status.

I believe that Michael Jackson draws a sense of normalcy from interacting with children. It's hard to imagine how it feels to be forced to live in a plastic bubble, unable to do what average people do or go where average people go without being mugged by star crazed fans. I believe that Michael Jackson's relationship with children is simply a need that we all have—to be treated like a normal human being. Children are very capable of not letting who you are interfere with their desire to play and have a good time with no strings attached.

Michael Jackson has had to contend with so much false publicity from the media, trying to expose him as being abnormal or some type of freak, that he does not trust very many people outside of his immediate family. Strangely enough, the only people that he did trust, were open to media bashing. There were always unsubstantiated write-ups in the major newspapers and tabloids speculating about the children Michael Jackson befriended and their relationships. Michael Jackson set the record straight in a 90-minute interview with Oprah Winfrey. He denied most of the rumors that the newspapers had been writing about him on several issues and relationships.

Michael Jackson's sister, Janet, was quoted as saying that Michael Jackson's flaw was not giving interviews and going on talk shows, which would have allowed the public a chance to get to know the real Michael Jackson.

One of the media's main areas of misunderstanding about Michael Jackson at the time was why he never married. The child molestation allegations were a welcomed answer to that question. Obviously, if you are not married or never married, you must be gay or a child molester—right? Wrong!

In the world we live in, you are either heterosexual (love the opposite sex), bisexual (prefer both sexes) or gay (prefers one's own sex). In the Christian world there is a fourth category called "chaste" (innocent of unlawful intercourse; celibate or abstinent). In order to keep the laws of God, a Christian is not allowed to have a sexual relationship with anyone other than their spouse. Sex outside of marriage is fornication and is considered sin in God's eyes. It may not make the six o'clock news, but there are a lot of Christians who obey these Biblical laws and refrain from having sex until they are married. Not to mention, there are some Christians that take a vow of abstinence. They vow to remain unmarried and commit their life to do the work of God. Most Priests and Nuns make this vow. I'm not saying that Michael Jackson made this type of vow, but he certainly has been about devoting his life to doing the work of God by helping underprivileged children around the world.

Michael Jackson has always acknowledged and referenced God in his life. He has lived a modeled life-style of Godliness. His humanitarian actions and deeds tap into the very heart of God—to help someone in need, to feed the poor, to do for the least and to walk in humility. These characteristics are the very characteristics of Godliness. "He loved the whole world that he gave.... his only begotten son." "Jesus came and gave his life so mankind could live." The Bible says "there is no greater gift than for a man to lay down his life for another."

It never bothered me that Michael Jackson was not married, especially after seeing the movie about his family, *The American Dream*. In it, there was a scene where Michael Jackson's oldest brother, Jackie, first announced that he was engaged while the group was at the height of their early career. Michael Jackson's response was, "how can you do that to our fans." Michael Jackson felt that getting married was somehow letting down his loving and adoring fans. When he gets out on the stage to perform, he takes his fans on a musical ecstasy—tantalizing their every fantasy, including the idea of him being every girls' dream. If only just for a moment.

After the child molestation allegations had been ongoing for several months, Michael Jackson spoke candidly to the world in a televised statement broadcast live from his Neverland Ranch on December 22, 1993. He informed millions of people worldwide of how he had suffered at the hands of the Santa Barbara County Sheriff's Department by being subjected to a body search where they took pictures of his body and examined and inspected his private parts. They were searching for corroborating evidence where the boy had given the police a description of Michael Jackson's body, including his genitals. It was later revealed that the authorities were not able to corroborate the boy's statements concerning Michael Jackson's body.

Michael Jackson called this action by the Santa Barbara County Sheriff's Department, "dehumanizing," "humiliating," and "the most humiliating ordeal of my life." He added that he endured this humiliation so it would prove his innocence. In other words, he could have refused the body search. He underwent the humiliation and shame of the body search being completely confident that he had nothing to hide and they had nothing to find. He continued in his statement, "I have only tried to help thousands upon thousands of children to live happy lives. It brings tears to my eyes when I see any child who suffers. I am not guilty of these allegations. But if I am guilty of anything, it is of giving all that I have to give to help children all over the world. It is of loving children, of all ages and races, it is of gaining sheer joy from seeing children with their innocent and smiling faces. It is of enjoying, through them, the childhood that I missed myself. If I am guilty of anything, it is of believing what God said about suffering little children to come unto Me and forbid them not, for such is the kingdom of heaven."

Part 3
The Plot Thickens

3.1
The 20 Million Dollar Demand

Dr. Chandler first brought his accusations of child molestation to his ex-wife, June Schwartz, at a school function in June of 1993. She reportedly didn't want to hear it. June thought very highly of Michael Jackson and thought he was a very kind person.

Dr. Chandler also discussed his plans with Dave Schwartz in a conversation that was secretly recorded by Mr. Schwartz. Dr. Chandler admitted to Mr. Schwartz that he had been "rehearsed about what to say" and as mentioned earlier, that "there were other people involved that are waiting for my phone call that are in certain positions... everything's going according to a certain plan that isn't just mine." Dr. Chandler admitted to Mr. Schwartz that, "if I don't get what I want, it will be a massacre." It was also in this telephone conversation that Dr. Chandler admitted that, "everything was going according to a certain plan," — "that isn't just mine."

During this time, Mr. Rothman and Dr. Chandler talked on the phone at least 3 to 5 times per day. Dr. Chandler did not come to the office very often at this point, but called constantly. Mr. Rothman always took Dr. Chandler's call behind closed doors. I thought it odd that after their many conversations there were never any memos to file, nothing memorializing or reiterating their many conversations.

— Geraldine Hughes —

As previously stated, on Wednesday, August 4, 1993, Dr. Chandler, his 13-year old son, Mr. Pellicano and Michael Jackson all met at the Westwood Marquis Hotel to discuss Dr. Chandler's allegations. It was at this meeting that Dr. Chandler made his intentions known to Michael Jackson concerning his twenty million dollar demand in exchange for not going public with his allegations of child molestation. It must be noted that Dr. Chandler did execute his plan after Michael Jackson failed to pay the twenty million dollars demanded. Also note that Dr. Chandler never publicly announced his suspicion of child molestation against Michael Jackson. The information was leaked to the media after the psychiatrist made a child sexual abuse report to the Department of Children's Services.

Dr. Chandler stated in his conversation with Mr. Schwartz that he was prepared to go forward with, "evidence that he claimed he had on Jackson." At the August 4, 1993 meeting with Mr. Pellicano and Michael Jackson, the only evidence Dr. Chandler had against Michael Jackson was a letter from Dr. Abrams giving Mr. Rothman advice about a hypothetical question that he queried him on previously and Dr. Chandler's mere, "threat of going public" with that advice. Dr. Chandler used this as a bargaining tool to demand twenty million dollars from Michael Jackson to keep quiet. When the meeting broke up, Mr. Pellicano said Dr. Chandler pointed his finger at Michael Jackson and said, **"I'm going to ruin you!"**

For those that need more information, more is on the way. In the meantime read this... Definition: *Blackmail* - to extort by threats of public exposure or criminal prosecution.

3.2
Negotiations Halted!

It is my guess that if Michael Jackson were guilty of the allegations, he would have paid the amount requested and this information would not have come to the public's attention. Instead, Michael Jackson, armed with a professional team of lawyers and investigators, conducted himself as one would who was not only innocent, but disgusted at the mere allegation of child molestation. Michael Jackson had to have been so disgusted with the allegation of child abuse that he was willing to stand firm and endure the humiliation of the allegations just to keep his accusers from succeeding with their scheme.

Immediately after the August 4, 1993 meeting, Mr. Rothman began negotiating with Mr. Pellicano for a screenplay writer offer which initially consisted of five million dollars for four screenplay writing deals. Mr. Pellicano and Mr. Rothman continually made phone calls back and forth discussing the details of what would be acceptable for each of their clients. Mr. Rothman was very careful not to say too much over the phone because of Mr. Pellicano's reputation of being able to record telephone conversations.

The negotiations then shifted to Mr. Rothman's office on August 9th between Mr. Rothman and Mr. Pellicano. I recall Mr. Pellicano coming to our office, but the meeting took place behind closed doors. It was later reported that this was the meeting in which Mr. Rothman expressed Dr. Chandler's request for a twenty million dollar movie deal.

Mr. Pellicano responded to Mr. Rothman's request via fax stating that their client, Michael Jackson, had done nothing wrong and therefore they would not consider paying the twenty million dollars requested. He did, however, express a willingness to assist the father's business venture by giving him a $350,000 screenwriting deal. He specifically said the offer was being made to resolve the custody dispute and to allow Dr. Chandler a chance to spend time with his son. (This was to overturn Dr. Chandler's accusation that Michael Jackson was destroying his relationship with his son by spending too much time with him and causing Dr. Chandler to lose his son's affection). This was the only claim that Michael Jackson was willing to take responsibility for because in his heart and soul, this was the only thing he may have been guilty of.

In another meeting which took place on August 13th 1993 in Mr. Rothman's office with Mr. Pellicano, Mr. Rothman counter offered for three screenplay writing deals. He gave Mr. Pellicano an ultimatum for three screenplays or nothing. Mr. Pellicano's counteroffer was for $350,000, which he said was made to help resolve the custody dispute and give Dr. Chandler an opportunity to work together with his son on the screenplays. I was able to read the letter Mr. Pellicano wrote to Mr. Rothman, stating this was his client's intention for making the counteroffer.

Mr. Pellicano stated from the beginning that this entire allegation of child molestation was about money. Although they were willing to negotiate with Mr. Rothman to appease Dr. Chandler's claim of losing time with his son, and allowing him and his son an opportunity to work together on a movie deal, he was not going to allow Dr. Chandler to make Michael Jackson the victim of extortion.

I cannot help but speculate that had Michael Jackson gone to trial and not settled this case with Dr. Chandler, he could have won. Mainly because, in my opinion, there was more evidence collected by Michael Jackson's attorneys and investigators to prove the extortion charges than the police had to show that any type of molestation ever took place. (Later, in the chapter titled: Legally Speaking, I will discuss in detail why Michael Jackson's decision to settle the case and pay the settlement amount to his accuser had nothing to do with his guilt or innocence.)

Mr. Rothman was very firm in this particular meeting and insisted that it was either the twenty million dollar deal or nothing. As mentioned before, Mr. Pellicano stormed out of Mr. Rothman's office and I could hear him say, "No way," and "that's extortion." Mr. Pellicano had a: *go for what you know*, or *shoot your best shot*, attitude towards Mr. Rothman.

This was the final meeting concerning the settlement negotiations in which Dr. Chandler was seeking financial compensation from Michael Jackson in exchange for not going public with his allegation of child molestation. Dr. Chandler was confident that being armed with a hypothetical letter of advice that was solicited by Mr. Rothman from a reputable psychiatrist, and the threat of going public with this humiliating allegation, was enough to move forward.

3.3
The Custody Battle

Dr. Evan Chandler and June Chandler divorced in 1985 due to a series of problems in their marriage. June Chandler received sole custody of their son, while Dr. Chandler was ordered to pay five hundred dollars a month in child support. Both June and Evan later remarried, and at the time of the child molestation allegations appeared to be sharing custody of their son without any problems.

As mentioned before... Michael Jackson met the Chandler boy, a friendship developed and Michael Jackson began spending a lot of time with the boy, his step-sister and mother at his Neverland Ranch. His mother, June Schwartz (June Chandler), admired Michael Jackson and did not have a problem with their friendship. In the beginning, Dr. Chandler did not mind sharing the affection of his son with the superstar, but after a while, the relationship between his son and Michael Jackson appeared to begin to take its toll when the 13-year old boy started spending more time with Michael Jackson than Dr. Chandler.

Dr. Chandler encouraged Michael Jackson to start spending time with the boy at his house. It began to appear as if he wanted a piece of the action as well. It was reported that Dr. Chandler asked Michael Jackson to build an extension on his house, a request that Michael Jackson considered. When Michael Jackson's request to build an addition onto his home ran into difficulty from the zoning department, Dr. Chandler boldly suggested that Michael Jackson simply build him a new house elsewhere.

The relationship between Michael Jackson and Dr. Chandler was becoming strained because of Dr. Chandler's threats. (More on the threats later.) For a short time after this, Michael Jackson began to withdraw from visiting the boy at Dr. Chandler's home. Dr. Chandler, in the recorded phone conversation with Dave Schwartz, reported he didn't know why Michael Jackson had stopped visiting him.

On the other hand, Michael Jackson's relationship with the Chandler boy and his mother continued to flourish. The boy, his step-sister and mother began traveling with him and were going to accompany Michael Jackson on his *Dangerous Tour*. Dr. Chandler became furious when he got word of this news. Some say that Dr. Chandler was furious because he was being cut out of the relationship with his son and Michael Jackson.

Dr. Chandler told Mr. Schwartz, in the recorded phone conversation, that he was mad at Michael for breaking up his family. He also admitted that he told Michael Jackson exactly what he wanted out of the deal.

It was at this point that Dr. Chandler hired Barry Rothman. It appears to me that if custody was the main issue he should have hired a family law attorney. Mr. Rothman was primarily known as an entertainment attorney, but had recently handled a child abuse case in which a female client accused the father of child molestation. Please note that Mr. Rothman, once again, represented the accuser.

In order for Dr. Chandler to carry out his plan, he needed custody of his 13-year old son. It would have been difficult to carry out such a plan without full custody or with interference from the child's mother.

In July 1993, Bertram Fields of Greenberg, Glusker, Fields, Claman & Machtinger, who was Michael Jackson's attorney, acted as an intermediary between June Schwartz and Barry Rothman during the custody battle between Dr. Chandler and his former wife, June Schwartz. Mr. Fields stated that he did not represent either party, but was merely carrying messages back and forth between them.

Dr. Chandler wanted June Schwartz to let him have custody of their 13-year old son for one week, beginning on July 12, 1993. Mr. Rothman promised June Schwartz that her 13-year old son could be picked up at Dr. Chandler's home on the evening of July 18, 1993 and returned to her custody. June Schwartz did not trust her former husband and was reluctant to honor his request. Only after Mr. Rothman had given his word to Mr. Fields, *as a fellow attorney*, that Dr. Chandler would live up to his commitment and return the boy on the evening of July 18, 1993, did June Schwartz allow Dr. Chandler to have custody of their son for the week.

On July 12, 1993, immediately after gaining custody of his 13-year old son, Dr. Chandler demanded that June Schwartz sign a stipulation prepared by Mr. Rothman. (A stipulation is a legal document that binds the parties to the terms specified and mutually agreed upon as set forth therein.) The stipulation stated that— 1) June Schwartz would not take their minor son from the County of Los Angeles without the prior written consent of Dr. Chandler; if she did she would do so in writing, setting forth where the minor will be taken, how long he will be gone, and who he would be with. 2) It allowed June Schwartz two days visitation per week based upon the terms and conditions that she not allow their 13-year old son to have contact or communication with Michael Jackson. 3) That if June Schwartz violated this term and condition, her visitation with her son would be limited and require supervised visitation, which she would bear the cost. 4) That all outstanding child support obligations from Dr. Chandler be deemed paid in full and that no further child support be required as long as he maintained full physical custody of their 13-year old child.

On the evening of July 18, 1993, Dr. Chandler failed to return the custody of the 13-year old boy to his former wife as he had promised, despite Mr. Rothman's word *as a fellow attorney*. He also ignored her repeated requests to return their son to her custody.

— REDEMPTION —

It appeared as if Dr. Chandler was holding his 13-year old son hostage from his mother when he presented her with the stipulation. June Schwartz stated that she signed the stipulation, as unreasonable as it was, because Dr. Chandler told her that if she didn't sign it he would not return their son to her custody. Ironically, even though June Schwartz signed the stipulation on July 12, 1993, Dr. Chandler still did not return the 13-year old boy, as he had promised, on July 18, 1993.

On August 16, 1993, Mr. Rothman received a call from June Schwartz's attorney advising him that an Ex Parte hearing would be held on August 17, 1993, demanding the immediate return of the 13-year old boy to her custody. As of that date, Dr. Chandler had custody of the 13-year old boy for one month and five days. He had ample opportunity to carry out the threats previously mentioned to Mr. Schwartz.

3.4
The Surprise Motion

An Ex Parte motion is an emergency hearing which the Court places on its calendar to be heard the next day. It only requires notification by telephone to all the concerned parties, and opposition paperwork must be served on the parties in the courtroom and argued before a Judge during the hearing.

Ex Parte Motions allow both parties to present a memorandum of points and authorities, which presents the Judge with established laws and past cases—referred to as precedents. In other words, standards, guides and patterns. An Ex Parte Motion also allows both parties to submit a declaration, which is a signed affidavit under oath, containing pertinent facts pertaining to the action that is before him/her, along with exhibits that can offer proof of the submitted statements.

On August 16, 1993, the law office of Freeman and Golden, June Schwartz's attorneys, called the law office of Barry Rothman and informed him that they would be appearing in court the very next day to obtain an Ex Parte order demanding the immediate return of the 13-year old Chandler boy. This motion filed by June Schwartz's attorney must have caught Mr. Rothman and Dr. Chandler off guard—it obviously was not a part of their plan and must have placed them in a panic as to how to deal with it.

I feel it's worth mentioning that attorneys are like doctors; they specialize in certain areas of law. Mr. Rothman, being an entertainment attorney, which primarily deals with contracts and negotiations, was lacking in the area of litigation skills.

— REDEMPTION —

Because Mr. Rothman was not a litigation attorney, he simply responded to the Ex Parte Motion by filing a declaration on behalf of Dr. Chandler. There were no points and authorities in the declaration giving the Judge legal grounds for their position, nor did it include anything to defend their position. More importantly, there was no mention whatsoever about any suspicion on Dr. Chandler's part in regards to his 13-year old son having been sexually molested by Michael Jackson. (There was absolutely no mention of child sexual abuse in the response to the motion.)

A real case of child molestation would have caused any normal parent to simply pick up the telephone and call the police or the child abuse hotline. Giving Dr. Chandler the benefit of the doubt in not doing what a normal parent would have done, the second course of action would have been to seek an order from the Court for custody that would guarantee the safety of his son. I know of no Judge anywhere who would not have granted Dr. Chandler an order for custody had he made any mention of sexual molestation in his response to June Schwartz's Ex Parte Motion.

When Mr. Rothman filed the declaration in response to June Schwartz's Ex Parte Motion on August 16, 1993, Dr. Chandler had already been negotiating with Michael Jackson since August 4, 1993, for money in exchange for not going public with his suspicion of child molestation.

This point, however, speaks for itself. Let me break it down and make it more easily understood. The Ex Parte Motion filed by June Schwartz caught Dr. Chandler and Mr. Rothman by surprise because they had not anticipated for it in their plan. (She had thrown them a curve ball.... as Dr. Chandler had admitted "we were moving according to a plan.") Because it required immediate response and attention, they were not prepared to adequately deal with such a crucial issue on the spur of the moment.

The fact that the declaration filed by Mr. Rothman in response to June Schwartz's Ex Parte Motion did not mention anything about Dr. Chandler's suspicion of child molestation validates, in my mind, that they were indeed moving according to a certain plan, because that would have been the perfect opportunity for Dr. Chandler and Mr. Rothman to officially bring up the issue of child molestation if they wanted to make certain his son was safe. (It appeared that Dr. Chandler was holding off on reporting his allegations as part of the plan.)

When someone calls the child protection hotline and reports an incident of child abuse, they immediately assign a social worker who comes to interview the child and family. If a determination is made on the part of the social worker that the child is in danger of any type of abuse, the worker will immediately remove the child and place him, or her, in protective custody. The law requires that a hearing is set within 48 hours, giving the parents an opportunity to be heard and recommendations to be made by the social worker. Either way, it all still leads back to the court system where a determination as to what is in the best interest of the child will be made.

As a result of Dr. Chandler and Mr. Rothman not supplying the Judge with any evidence or information in the declaration stating they had good reason to keep custody of the 13-year old boy, the Court ordered, forthwith, (immediately) that Dr. Chandler return custody of his son back to June Schwartz.

The Court also ordered the stipulation that Dr. Chandler insisted June Schwartz sign be overturned. Dr. Chandler lost the Ex Parte Motion and the Court ordered him to return the 13-year old child to June Schwartz's custody forthwith.

After being ordered to return the custody of the 13-year boy old to June Schwartz, instead of obeying the Court's order, Dr. Chandler, instead, took the boy to see the psychiatrist, who then reported the child abuse on the same day of the Ex Parte Motion hearing—August 17, 1993. It was only days after Dr. Chandler took his 13-year old son to the psychiatrist that the child molestation allegations were leaked to the news media and became public knowledge.

3.5
Third Party Disclosure

A key element in this entire case for Dr. Chandler and Mr. Rothman, was *how to report* the child molestation allegations that he had admittedly planned to make public if Michael Jackson did not pay the twenty million dollar demand. In order for the accusation to be believable, it had to come from a reputable source. It was well know that Mr. Rothman's reputation was questionable, and from my observation of Dr. Chandler, he, too, did not have the courage to be the one responsible for accusing Michael Jackson of child molestation to a worldwide audience. Immediately his motive would have been under question and he had already done far too much in terms of negotiating for money to keep quiet concerning his allegation. If, however, you were truly a victim, you would not have to scheme or plot as how to report child abuse. Anyone with the knowledge or suspicion of child abuse has a right to call and report it to the Department of Children's Services.

According to my diary entry, and my memory, on July 27, 1993, I typed a letter to Dr. Chandler from Mr. Rothman advising him how to report child abuse through a third party without liability to the parent. I was extremely suspicious of this correspondence from Mr. Rothman, so much so that I noted its contents in my calendar book diary. The letter from Mr. Rothman was brief and advised Dr. Chandler to see the enclosed. The enclosure was documentation explaining how to report child abuse without liability to the parent. It had a lot of corresponding Penal Codes, Civil Procedures and Civil

Codes. Knowing I could not photocopy the letter, I wrote down the codes so I could look them up at a later date. The codes consisted of:

Penal Code section 11165, 11166, 11172

Code of Civil Procedures: 516 "Parents Right to Injuries"

Civil Code: 49 "Enticement of Parent"

Civil Code: 4600.5, 4608 "Joint custody, legal custody, determination of the best interest of the child"

Mr. Rothman sent the letter to Dr. Chandler on July 27, 1993, the negotiations for the movie deal were held on August 4th 1993, and the boy was taken to the psychiatrist on August 17th 1993. If you recall, in Dr. Chandler's recorded conversation with Mr. Dave Schwartz, which was recorded prior to July 9th, 1993, Dr. Chandler admitted that there were other people involved... waiting for his phone call. That he had paid them to do it. Everything was going according to a certain plan that it wasn't just his. And that once that he made a phone call, that guy (Rothman) was going to destroy everybody in sight in any devious, nasty, cruel way that he could do it... and that he had given him full authority to do so. Dr. Chandler also admitted, "There's no way I can lose. I've checked that inside out."

Dr. Chandler made it look like he simply took his son to a psychiatrist and it was the psychiatrist that stumbled upon the child molestation allegations. Nothing was further from the truth. Taking his son to the psychiatrist was well thought out and calculated because Dr. Chandler had received detailed information from Mr. Rothman about the ramifications of using a third party to report child abuse.

— REDEMPTION —

WHEN THE NEGOTIATIONS BETWEEN ROTHMAN AND JACKSON CAME TO A HALT, AND THE COURT ORDERED DR. CHANDLER TO RETURN HIS 13-YEAR OLD SON BACK TO JUNE SCHWARTZ'S CUSTODY, DR. CHANDLER TOOK HIS SON TO THE PSYCHIATRIST WITH ROTHMAN'S FULL KNOWLEDGE, COACHING AND INSTRUCTION.

Mr. Rothman advised Dr. Chandler as how to report child abuse through a third party and without liability to a parent. The Codes that Mr. Rothman supplied Dr. Chandler explained in great detail all the ramifications of reporting child abuse/molestation, how the law would determine what was in the best interest of the child and a parent's right to injuries; and through a third party who was reputable, believable and by someone who would effectively make the reporting of said allegations look credible.

When Mr. Schwartz asked Dr. Chandler if that helped his son, Dr. Chandler's response was, "That's irrelevant to me. It's going to be bigger than all of us put together. The whole thing is going to crash down on everybody and destroy everybody in sight. It will be a massacre if I don't get what I want."

There is no doubt in my mind that Dr. Chandler did exactly what he said he was going to do. After reading this far, are there still any doubts in yours?

3.6
The Allegations Launched!

To recap... when the court ordered Dr. Chandler to return the custody of the boy to his former wife, June Schwartz, and denied his request for a restraining order against Michael Jackson, Dr. Chandler took the 13-year old boy to see the psychiatrist who reported the child abuse charges against Michael Jackson. It is important to note that Dr. Chandler would not have done this had Michael Jackson paid him the money; since after paying him the money in the settlement, Dr. Chandler dropped all charges against Michael Jackson. Could this have been the *plan* that Dr. Chandler referred to in his recorded conversation with Mr. Dave Schwartz? It appears that once the money was paid, it brought an end to the child molestation allegations by Dr. Chandler.

In the recorded conversation between Dr. Chandler and Mr. Schwartz, Dr. Chandler admitted out of his own mouth that he had a *plan* and that things were going according to a *certain plan* and all he had to do was make a phone call. He also revealed that he had hired people to, "move against Jackson." He admitted that he had paid them to do it. He further admitted that the plan wasn't just his. He stated that after making a call, someone was going to destroy everybody in sight in any devious, nasty, cruel way that he can do it. This was the profile that Dr. Chandler painted of Mr. Rothman who was, at that time, guiding Dr. Chandler every step of the way before, during and after the child molestation allegations.

— REDEMPTION —

The definition of *plan* is: To devise, scheme, plot, intend, a method devised for doing something or attaining an end.

The definition of *extortion* is: To obtain from a person by force or undue or illegal power or ingenuity.

The definition of *ingenuity* is: Skill or cleverness in devising... Inventiveness. An ingenuous device.

Another incriminating statement that Dr. Chandler admitted in his own words was, that he had been rehearsed about what to say and not to say. This means that someone else was advising him and giving him instructions.

What exactly was Dr. Chandler referring to as his *plan*? False child abuse charges, however, are well known for being a scheme, device or plot, especially during a custody battle between parents. It is reported as the number one tactic in child custody battles. Again... remember, Dr. Chandler took his 13-year old son to the psychiatrist on the same day that he was ordered to return the child back to his mother. I am familiar enough with the court structure to know that it would not have denied Dr. Chandler's restraining order and custody request if there was any mention of sexual abuse anywhere in his court papers. The Court would have protected the safety of the child if it had any information that the child was being harmed in any way whatsoever, no matter who the offense was levied against. There would not have been any hesitation on the part of the Court to grant Dr. Chandler's request for custody and a restraining order, had the issue of sexual abuse been brought out in his paperwork. He had already made a claim of sexual abuse against Michael Jackson at the time of presenting his opposition paperwork, however, remember, there was no mention of sexual abuse in his opposition papers filed with the Court. Any other attorney with that knowledge beforehand would have used the sexual abuse issue as a primary basis for requesting custody and a restraining order. In this case, however, Dr. Chandler and Mr. Rothman failed to bring sexual abuse charges to the Court's attention even though, at that time, the accusation was already made to Michael Jackson's attorneys and investigators.

Instead of returning his 13-year old son to his former wife, pursuant to the court order, Dr. Chandler rushed his son to the psychiatrist where the child molestation allegations were made. This tactic of Dr. Chandler's was completely overlooked and unmentioned by millions of experts, Americans, tabloids, and the news media around the world. Why didn't anyone notice the timing of these two events as a possible clue that, taking the boy to a psychiatrist was all a part of the *plan* that Dr. Chandler had made previously referenced?

Although the reporting of the child abuse allegation was of greater concern to Mr. Rothman and Dr. Chandler, they did not count on June Schwartz's attorney filing the Ex Parte papers requesting the immediate return of her son. This Ex Parte hearing required them to show up in court within 24 hours of receiving notice of the hearing, and, having an explanation as to why her motion should not be granted. Every diabolical scheme has a quirk in it. Well, I believe this was the quirk in Dr. Chandler's and Mr. Rothman's plan. June Schwartz had just thrown a wrench in her former husband's and Mr. Rothman's supposed perfect plan. They had to think quickly to counter the unexpected flaw to get back on track. They had to come up with a counter move that would offset hers. Because an Ex Parte hearing requires the case to be heard on shortened notice to the parties involved, it does not give the opposing party much time to figure out their rebuttal.

On August 23, 1993, I was watching TV in the conference room while on break at Mr. Rothman's office. There was a special news break referring to Michael Jackson. That's when I, and the entire world, learned of the child molestation allegations that had been made against Michael Jackson. I am sure that from the world's point of view this news report came as a complete shock. I was shocked for a different reason. I knew instantly while watching the news report that the child abuse allegation against Michael Jackson was false. I had no doubt whatsoever of Michael Jackson's innocence from the very beginning of this ordeal.

3.7
The Child Molestation Investigation

On August 17, 1993, the child molestation investigation began with the Los Angeles Police Department serving search warrants on Michael Jackson's Neverland Ranch. Michael Jackson had gone to Bangkok, Thailand to begin his *Dangerous World Tour* and was not there during the search of his home. During the search, several boxes of photographs and videotapes were removed from the premises.

On August 21, 1993, the Police Department served a search warrant on Michael Jackson's Century City condo. The Los Angeles Police Department came under immediate attack as to how they were able to obtain the search warrants based solely on the allegations of one 13-year old boy. The police are normally required to have probable cause that a crime has been committed before they can obtain a search warrant from a Judge.

Michael Jackson's phone book was confiscated and the police contacted just about everyone in it to question them about alleged wrongdoing by Michael Jackson. The 13-year old boy also provided the police with the names of other boys that he claimed were molested by Michael Jackson. The police investigated every lead and every child that was alleged to have been molested. They even began to interrogate Michael Jackson's friends, family, employees and former employees.

Once the news of the investigation surfaced, it was quickly known that the tabloids were paying big bucks for anyone to come forth with any information, whether true or not. People began to come out of the woodwork with so-called eye witness stories of inappropriate behavior. None of this information was reported prior to the allegations being made public.

Allegedly the Los Angeles Police Department proved to be the greatest leak of confidential documents from the Department of Children's Services, which contained the details of the child molestation allegations.

The police investigation was reportedly attempting to dig up witnesses, even at the cost of lying to the boys they interviewed. Michael Jackson's then attorney, Bertram Fields, wrote a letter to Police Chief Willie Williams advising him, "That your officers have told frightened youngsters outrageous lies, such as, "we have nude photos of you," to push them into making accusations against Michael Jackson. There are, of course, no such photos of these youngsters, and they have no truthful allegations to make. But the officers appeared ready to employ any device to generate potential evidence against Mr. Jackson. Chief Williams' response was a standard not willing to admit guilt answer, "We stand behind our officers."

After a long and costly investigation, which produced no evidence, the police resorted to even more desperate measures. On March 17, 1994, Katherine Jackson, Michael Jackson's mother, was subpoenaed to testify before the grand jury in Los Angeles. It is not normal procedure for a mother to be called to testify against her own son. Many individuals spoke out of their disbelief that the investigation had stooped to such tactics. Howard Weitzman stated, "In all the years of my experience, I've never before seen the mother of the target of an investigation called before the grand jury. It's just done in real poor taste. It borders on harassment."

Another of Michael Jackson's attorney, Richard Steingard, stated to the press, "A prosecutor attempting or trying to use a mother against a son, a parent against a child is just wholly inappropriate and even more so inappropriate in this case because Mrs. Jackson has repeatedly and publicly denounced the allegations and insisted that her son was innocent."

Thomas Sneddon, District Attorney from the Santa Barbara County, and Gil Garcetti, District Attorney from the Los Angeles County, launched separate investigations into the child molestation allegations. Although, the investigation actively lasted for approximately 13 months and remained open for six years, neither Mr. Sneddon nor Mr. Garcetti were able to make a case against Michael Jackson. Mr. Garcetti blamed it on the little boy's refusal to testify after reaching a settlement. Although it is a well known fact that if they had more than one witness who could testify to sexual wrongdoings by Michael Jackson, they would have indicted Michael Jackson. As often happens in high profile cases, too much taxpayer money was spent and the police needed justification because of it.

After coming up empty handed, Garcetti sought to change the California law that does not require juveniles to testify in sex abuse cases. Simply put, the only witness he had against Michael Jackson was the little boy, and because of the then state laws, he could not be forced to testify.

This is not meant to be demeaning to the authorities, because I thoroughly realize that our police officers put their lives on the line daily to keep peace in our land. They face constant dangers from notorious criminals everyday. Even in light of the recent discovery of wrongdoings by the hands of police officers, and probably even more cases than have been revealed, there still remain many cases of an abuse of power at the hands of law enforcement personnel. This includes not only police officers, but the officers of parole, probation, jail and youth authority personnel, and immigration officers. As most of us have experienced in one form or another, anyone that has authority over someone else's life, experiences the temptation of abusing power associated with that authority.

Mr. Garcetti appeared to be very single-minded in his manner of pursuit of trying to indict Michael Jackson on the charge of child molestation. I am not criticizing Mr. Garcetti's approach or pursuit, but in the interest of justice, there has to be an equal manner of pursuit to protect innocent parties from being framed or railroaded into being charged with offenses they did not commit. This case was unfortunate to me because when it came to the investigation of extortion, Mr. Garcetti's office did not provide that same manner of pursuit to Michael Jackson as it did for Dr. Chandler. Obvious facts were overlooked — I was an employee of Mr. Rothman's office and no one from Mr. Garcetti's office subpoenaed me to investigate the extortion charge.

Not being able to indict Michael Jackson after such a heated pursuit was an embarrassment to the District Attorney's office. It appeared to many as if Mr. Garcetti was waging a personal vendetta against Michael Jackson. The District Attorney's office spent millions of tax payers dollars trying to indict him of the charge of child abuse. This reminds me of the O.J. Simpson case, and while I have your attention, I might as well insert my theory on that case. I contend that there are only TWO people who know whether O.J. Simpson did or did not kill his wife and Rod Goldman; O.J. and God. All others are merely guessing. That is another case that I firmly believe was not given enough critical thinking or equal analogy for the possibility of innocence or being framed.

The child abuse charges against Michael Jackson were never formally closed. Instead of closing the case after a failure to come up with enough credible evidence to indict Michael Jackson, Mr. Garcetti simply stated that the investigation would remain open until the six year statute of limitation ran out.

Part 4
The Aftermath

4.1
The Media Goes Wild

It goes without saying that instantly after the news reported the child molestation accusations against Michael Jackson, the news media went wild. At Mr. Rothman's office the telephone started ringing off the wall, with calls from every news media and tabloid magazine from all over the world. I remember calls from London based tabloids and news agencies wanting information. News personalities came to our door wanting to talk to Mr. Rothman concerning the allegations. Mr. Rothman denied all phone calls and talked to no one concerning the allegations. Their every effort and attempt to get a story, a comment or a statement concerning the allegations were denied. Our office did not give statements to anyone.

Likewise, the news media tried to locate Dr. Chandler and his son to get a statement from them. They were not prepared for the frenzy that fell on their doorstep. Frantically, they took cover at Mr. Rothman's office and camped out over night. While the news media was looking for them at home, they never thought to look for them in Mr. Rothman's office.

The media did not stop trying to get a statement from Mr. Rothman's office. The telephone rang constantly, the receptionist was told to say that we had no comment. News crews showed up at our door with cameras ready to capture anything. On occasions, Mr. Rothman would go to the door and rudely tell them that they were trespassing and if they didn't leave he would call the police. They would just retreat to the hallway and wait to catch Mr. Rothman coming or going to try again to get a statement.

The media initially learned of the child molestation allegations when Dr. Abrams, the psychiatrist seeing the 13-year old boy, made a report to the Department of Children's Services after a three-hour therapy session with him. The Department of Children's Services contacted the police department and a search warrant was issued to search Michael Jackson's Neverland Ranch and Century City condominium. Immediately after the warrants were issued, the news leaked to the media and on August 23, 1993 the story broke in a special news report.

Within just a matter of hours, the allegations of child molestation was the top story on all major cable and network channels around the world. The conservative networks were airing news as soon as it came in and the tabloids were doing the same regardless whether the stories were true or not. Even the British newspapers were headlining the story across Great Britain. The tabloids were offering as high as a half a million dollars for information from anyone that would be willing to corroborate and authenticate the boy's allegations. They were not concerned about the story being true because many so-called witnesses came forth and their story was later struck down.

Because of the hype and media frenzy taking place, even highly confidential information was being leaked and flashed across the news media throughout the world. Even the details from the Department of Children's Services report were leaked to the press reporting the details of the allegations given to the social worker. This information is supposed to be highly confidential and not available to the general public.

I was totally disgusted during this entire ordeal as I watched the media try this case based on the word of only one young boy's allegation, which was never substantiated. Yet, the way the story was reported in the media, you would have thought they had a signed confession by Michael Jackson personally admitting to the allegations.

— REDEMPTION —

The law states that you are innocent until proven guilty. However, the media had Michael Jackson tried and convicted, and the world was buying the reports hook, line, sinker, bait, fishing pole, fishermen, sea and shore.

The media was interviewing people claiming to have witnessed Michael Jackson exercising inappropriate behavior with children who had visited his Neverland Ranch. Most of the witnesses who came forward were ex-employees, such as maids and bodyguards that had worked for Michael Jackson and had either quit or been fired. The police even flew to the Philippines to interview two ex-employees who claimed to have a diary of events that happened at the Neverland Ranch documenting inappropriate behavior by Michael Jackson with children that visited his Neverland Ranch.

Every witness that came forward made headline news. Every detail of the investigation was reported and printed in the tabloids. It appeared to me that the news media was more favorable to the witnesses claiming to have damaging information because this gave them the spotlight in their reporting. However, when the witnesses' claims turned out to be invalid, the media swept it under the rug. They never bothered to refute these so-called witnesses.

When all the smoke cleared and the dust had settled, the entire case boiled down to just one thing: the 13-year old boy's word against Michael Jackson's. After all the witnesses were interviewed, millions of dollars spent on the investigation and grand jury hearings, etc., the heart of this entire case was the boy's word against Michael Jackson's. No evidence or proof was ever offered, and no credible witness was ever presented.

4.2
What Reporters Were Dying To Know

While the news media and tabloids were having a field day with the numerous witnesses who were coming forth against Michael Jackson, not much was being reported from the Chandler camp. But there were a lot of interesting things taking place:

Bomb Threats: The phones were still ringing off the wall from news media and reporters. The office started receiving threatening phone calls directed at Mr. Rothman. One day we received a bomb threat. Of course, Mr. Rothman would not allow us to leave the office. Even Mr. Rothman began coming to the office with extreme caution. Right after receiving the bomb threat Mr. Rothman decided to take a weeks vacation. I was told that this was his first vacation in five years.

Chandler Stake Out: Right after the allegations hit the news media, everyone was looking for Dr. Chandler. The media found out where he lived and were staking out his residence. Dr. Chandler and the boy came to our office to take shelter. While everyone was looking for Dr. Chandler and his son, they were held up at our office. They spent the night in the conference room located just a few feet in front of my desk. To me Dr. Chandler appeared to be a nervous wreck. He paced back and forth and was biting everyone's head off. At one point I heard him yell at Mr. Rothman, "...It's my ass that's on the line and in danger of going to prison." (I noted this statement in my diary.)

The Attack: One morning Dr. Chandler called Mr. Rothman's office from the hospital. Mr. Rothman had not yet arrived at the office, and Dr. Chandler left a message stating that he needed to talk to Mr. Rothman as soon as he arrived. When Mr. Rothman arrived he called Dr. Chandler and was told that the night before someone approached him on the street while leaving his dental practice and attacked him for no apparent reason. The attack was severe enough that he was hospitalized for his injuries. It was assumed that the attacker was an angry Michael Jackson fan.

The Attorney Switch: When the investigation of the extortion charge against Mr. Rothman and Dr. Chandler began, both of them sought criminal representation. It was reported that Mr. Rothman was no longer Dr. Chandler's attorney. Behind the scenes, Dr. Chandler and Mr. Rothman continued to put their heads together as they very carefully planned their next moves. Dr. Chandler continued to call our office at least four to five times per day (on a light day) to speak with Mr. Rothman, and he continued to give Dr. Chandler advice concerning his every move. It seemed as if Dr. Chandler would not move without Mr. Rothman's direction and/or counsel. At this point, Mr. Rothman was totally immersed in assisting Dr. Chandler through their ordeal.

4.3
Secret Meetings

Immediately after the allegations became public, Mr. Rothman hosted numerous secret meetings at his office in the back conference room, located only a few feet away from my desk. All the meetings were behind closed doors, but they would always come up for air, sometimes leaving the door open. That's when I was able to hear outbursts and comments which led me to believe that the child molestation allegations were causing Dr. Chandler and Mr. Rothman a great deal of anxiety. The only one who appeared to be calm was the 13-year old boy.

While the news media was reporting the bitter custody battle between Dr. Chandler and June Schwartz, they were all meeting behind closed doors planning and strategizing. They were laughing and talking out loud. It appeared as if they had all joined forces to corroborate their efforts. It was during a behind-the-scenes meeting that I overheard Dr. Chandler say, "I almost had a twenty million dollar deal." (I noted this in my diary.) I don't know what prompted him to say this, but he yelled it loud and clear. This was also before the settlement talks commenced.

As one might imagine, the extortion investigation made Dr. Chandler and Mr. Rothman nervous. They were both required to go and speak with the investigator about the extortion charge. When that was made known, Rothman tried to reach Dr. Chandler all that day. When Dr. Chandler finally returned his call, Mr. Rothman took the call in the associate attorney's office near my desk. I overhead Mr. Rothman tell Dr. Chandler that they needed "to meet over the weekend" and talk before speaking to the investigator to "make sure our stories are the same." That was the reason for the emergency meeting that Mr. Rothman asked Dr. Chandler to make himself available over the weekend.

At this point Mr. Rothman was more nervous than careful. He seemed to forget that he was not in his office behind closed doors while having this conversation.

The secret meetings continued between Mr. Rothman and Dr. Chandler until the end of my employment. One afternoon Dr. Chandler came to Mr. Rothman's office late, approximately 5:45 P.M., 15 minutes before my shift ended and they immediately went into the conference room behind closed doors. There was something unusual about this particular meeting. The meeting lasted past my shift-end, so although I wanted to stay and find out what was going on, instead, I went home about 6:00 P.M.

I was extremely curious about the purpose for this impromptu meeting, so before I left I walked over to the door and tried to listen to their conversation. They were speaking in a low tone and I could not hear their conversation. I walked back to my computer, afraid someone would open the door and find me standing outside. I then got the courage to walk back over to the door and overheard Mr. Rothman telling Dr. Chandler in a loud voice that, "...we just have to stick to the plan... we cannot deviate from the plan."

4.4
The Extortion Investigation

Extortion on the part of an attorney warrants disbarment. Barton v. State Bar of California (1935) 40 P.2d 502, 2 C.2d 294.

Anthony Pellicano stated repeatedly to the news media that the entire child molestation allegation was an elaborate extortion scheme by Mr. Rothman and Dr. Chandler to extort money from Michael Jackson. Throughout the entire ordeal Mr. Pellicano never changed his opinion. In a declaration filed by Mr. Pellicano in opposition to a Motion for Trial Preference and in support of Michael Jackson's Motion for Stay of Discovery and Trial, he stated that Dr. Chandler and Mr. Rothman demanded twenty million dollars in the form of four—five million dollar payments for *writing deals* for Dr. Chandler's services. Mr. Pellicano further stated that Dr. Chandler said he would *ruin* Michael Jackson if he didn't get what he wanted and that he believed Dr. Chandler, directly or indirectly, found a way to make his claims public in retaliation for Michael Jackson not meeting his demand.

Michael Jackson's attorneys filed extortion charges against Dr. Chandler and Mr. Rothman. Dr. Chandler and Mr. Rothman took the extortion charges seriously; each hired criminal defense attorneys. The extortion investigation made both of them very nervous. The investigator called Mr. Rothman, wanting to meet with him separately regarding the case. Mr. Rothman tried to reach Dr. Chandler all day concerning the meeting with the investigator. When Dr. Chandler finally called to speak to Mr. Rothman, he took Dr. Chandler's call in the associate attorney's office located near my desk. I overhead Mr. Rothman tell Dr. Chandler that they needed to meet over the weekend and talk before speaking to the investigator to make sure their stories were the same. Mr. Rothman reiterated to Dr. Chandler that they needed to make sure they were both saying the same thing. Mr. Rothman insisted that Dr. Chandler meet with him over the weekend before the meeting with the investigator which was to take place, I believe it was that coming Monday. After hearing Mr. Rothman make this statement to Dr. Chandler, there was no question in my mind that Michael Jackson was the innocent victim of an elaborate extortion scheme.

Although the extortion investigation did not generate the same media attention as the child molestation allegations did, underneath the surface, Mr. Rothman and Dr. Chandler were sweating bullets. Mr. Rothman began to let his guard down and was not being as careful as he had previously been. It appeared as if he was starting to lose control of his temper.

The media, on the other hand, did not give the extortion charges the same intensity, air time, and news attention as it did the child molestation allegations. The investigation of the extortion charges was not handled in the same manner as the child molestation allegations. No witnesses were subpoenaed... at least it wasn't reported. There was no attention given as to whether or not search warrants were issued to search Dr. Chandler's and Mr. Rothman's home and office. They did not travel out of the country to investigate the extortion charges. All they did was investigate locally. Had the investigation of the extortion charges been as thorough as it was for the child molestation allegations, I would not be writing this book, giving the public information that should have already been reported.

4.5
Jackson Changes Attorneys

Bertram Fields was the lead attorney during the initial stages of the investigation. Michael Jackson asked him to intervene on his behalf when Dr. Chandler first started making accusations of child molestation. Bert Fields is one of the most prominent entertainment attorneys in the legal field. He negotiated the biggest music deal for Michael Jackson with Sony Records. However, when the criminal case started heating up, he brought Howard Weitzman on board, who is one of the top criminal attorneys in the legal field.

On November 23, 1993, Mr. Fields attempted to delay the trial in the child molestation case, by stating to a courtroom full of reporters that a criminal indictment was forthcoming against Michael Jackson. Mr. Weiztman publicly recanted Mr. Fields' statement saying that he "miss-spoke himself." However, Mr. Fields' reason for making such a statement was due to the fact that according to California and Federal laws, when a civil defendant faces the possibility of criminal prosecution for the same factual allegations, the defendant is entitled to a Stay of Discovery and Trial in civil proceedings until the statute of limitation has expired on the criminal case. Pacers, Inc. v. Superior Court, 162 Cal.App.3d 686, Cal.Rptr. 743 (1984).

Although Mr. Fields had a good reason for making this statement, it did not stop the Court's action in granting Mr. Feldman's request for Trial Preference and Motion to compel Michael Jackson's deposition. The Court also denied Mr. Fields' Motion to Stay Trial and Discovery. Soon after the defense suffered such a loss on all four motions, that would have at least delayed the civil trial until after the criminal trial was extinguished, Mr. Fields resigned as counsel for Michael Jackson. Shortly thereafter Mr. Pellicano resigned as well. Even though Mr. Fields and Mr. Pellicano resigned from the case, they both maintained their dignity and confidence in Michael Jackson's innocence.

With Weitzman in complete control of Michael Jackson's defense, he brought in one of the country's top civil and criminal attorneys, Johnnie Cochran Jr. Mr. Cochran gained worldwide notoriety as one of the legal attorneys in the O.J. Simpson murder trial (referred to as a member of "The Dream Team") in which O.J. was acquitted. Mr. Weitzman also brought in John Branca who was a former attorney that represented Michael Jackson in 1990.

The change of attorneys definitely affected the direction of the child molestation case. As you may recall, at the time that Mr. Fields and Mr. Pellicano were still in charge of Michael Jackson's defense, Michael Jackson was out of the country on tour and had just ended his tour claiming drug dependency, which may have been another delaying tactic. Dr. Chandler's civil attorney, Larry Feldman, had filed the civil lawsuit on September 14, 1993, and was trying desperately to take Michael Jackson's deposition, but no one could pinpoint Michael Jackson's whereabouts. The media portrayed this as Michael Jackson running away from the charges and that he was possibly never going to return to the United States to avoid prosecution. Others speculated he was having cosmetic surgery, altering parts of his body which the little boy may have been able to identify.

As soon as Mr. Weitzman and Mr. Cochran took control of the defense, Michael Jackson shortly thereafter resurfaced and returned home to the United States, stating that he was well and willing to proclaim his innocence. He also conducted several interviews and made exclusive public statements proclaiming his innocence and voicing his displeasure about the humiliating body search that he was forced to undergo by the authorities.

However, unlike Mr. Fields and Mr. Pellicano whom were adamant about defending Michael Jackson all the way to trial, Mr. Weitzman and Mr. Cochran immediately began talks about settlement. Mr. Fields and Mr. Pellicano were against settling with Dr. Chandler because they did not want him to get away with his extortion attempt. They were confident that they could win this case at trial. Their primary goal was to beat Dr. Chandler at trial.

Mr. Weitzman and Mr. Cochran, on the other hand, were in favor of settlement from the beginning to spare Michael Jackson the humiliation and pain of having his private life, which he holds dear, splashed across the nation on every network and cable news channel. Dr. Chandler's attorney had already started requesting financial statements from Michael Jackson's camp, disclosing all his assets.

The unfortunate aspect of changing attorneys and not going to trial was that all the initial investigation work that Mr. Fields and Mr. Pellicano had dug up never made its way into the courtroom. Mr. Pellicano had gathered incriminating evidence against Dr. Chandler and Mr. Rothman which could have won Michael Jackson a victorious outcome in court. However, Michael Jackson was not willing to endure the public scrutiny of his private life and affairs. It was my contention that had Michael Jackson gone to trial, he would have won. Mr. Fields and Mr. Pellicano had the ammunition to win!

However, Mr. Weitzman and Mr. Cochran did a marvelous job in taking control of the events that caused Michael Jackson to return to the United States to face the charges, not as a victim of drug addition, but as the victim of false child molestation charges being launched against him. With a new team of attorneys in place, Michael Jackson emerged with a different attitude and outlook.

4.6
The Settlement

A settlement means that all parties have mutually agreed upon terms to resolve the matter at hand without the need for a trial. Once a case settles and all the terms are carried out under the settlement, the case is over. It then releases all parties from future liabilities surrounding the case.

Immediately after Johnnie Cochran Jr. joined forces with Mr. Weitzman as associate counsel on December 13, 1993, it was stated that the talks of settlement began to surface. Some of the issues that more than likely factored into the decision to settle may have included the following:

Michael Jackson's defense had been unsuccessful in delaying the civil lawsuit and Discovery.

Michael Jackson's defense had lost their attempt to block Feldman's request for a speedy trial in this case and trial was scheduled to take place in March of 1994.

Mr. Cochran's request for a protective order to prevent all parties in action from disclosing informal and formal discovery material to the District Attorney's office to protect Michael Jackson's Fifth Amendment rights in the case of the criminal proceeding was denied.

The motion for a protective order brought a lot of legal controversy from the media, newspaper and District Attorneys office. All of whom seemed more interested portraying Michael Jackson in a negative way than getting at the truth.

There was the possibility that the civil trial could last anywhere from six months to several years.

Because of all the negative worldwide media coverage, Michael Jackson's chances of getting a fair trial became questionable.

For the millions of people who felt Michael Jackson was guilty because he settled and paid a large sum of money to the 13-year old boy, these are just a few things that were going on behind the scenes working against Michael Jackson. It was even reported that the *attorneys' reputations* were also a consideration for settling the case as opposed to going to trial and finding out who would be the losing attorney.

There was also the threat of Michael Jackson having to face double jeopardy in having to defend himself in the criminal case as well as the civil case, even though the law is clearly designed to prevent a defendant from having to be tried twice on the same issue at the same time. However, this did not seem to prevail in Michael Jackson's case. Even the Fifth Amendment, which provides that a person cannot be compelled in any criminal case to be a witness against himself, provides protection from being tried twice on the same issue. But even Michael Jackson's Fifth Amendment protection did not supercede a child's right to a speedy trial.

The District Attorney's office was also *laying in wait* to utilize the information that was going to be uncovered or revealed in the civil lawsuit for use in their criminal investigation. They made it very clear that they would request a copy of all depositions and discovery taken in this case for their use in prosecuting the criminal case against Michael Jackson.

On January 27, 1994 the civil complaint filed by Dr. Chandler's attorney, Larry Feldman, was dismissed. Michael Jackson settled the civil case for an undisclosed amount of money. The court ordered the terms of the settlement to be confidential and banned the attorneys, parties, and court personnel from mentioning the contents of said settlement proceedings. It was speculated, however, that the approximate amount of the settlement was twenty million dollars. It was estimated that Dr. Chandler received approximately one to two million dollars and the balance of the money was put in a trust fund for the little boy until he reached the age of 18. The parents were ordered to relinquish custody over the little boy's estate, and a retired judge was appointed guardian over his estate.

It has been speculated in recent news reports that Michael Jackson did not actually pay the little boy twenty million dollars, but in fact deposited twenty million dollars into a trust account in which he lives off of the interest. It was also reported that Michael Jackson may not have even paid the estimated twenty million dollars out of his own pocket but that he reported the loss to his insurance company and the money may have been paid through his insurance.

The terms of the settlement must have also included that Michael Jackson had to dismiss the extortion charges against Mr. Rothman and Dr. Chandler, since immediately after the settlement the charges were withdrawn.

It wasn't until I started shopping for a literary agent for my book that I discovered that many people believed Michael Jackson was guilty of the child molestation charges simply because he did, in fact, settle. I heard people say repeatedly, "if he was innocent, why did he settle?" I did not realize that was how a great majority of people felt. I assumed that people believed in the constitution of this country, which states you are innocent until proven guilty.

In the legal profession, settling a case is the most preferred way to resolve a dispute, mainly because of the escalating court costs involved in litigating a case. The longer it takes to resolve a court matter, the more money it costs the litigants and the taxpayers. The Prosecutors, District Attorneys and police are paid by the taxpayers, and they do not spare any costs in pursuing these cases, not to mention, the costs of expert witnesses, expensive attorneys fees, jury fees and court costs.

Cases sometimes make it all the way to the threshold of trial, and then settle right on the eve of trial. The settlement of a case, however, has never been recognized in the legal field as an admission of anyone's guilt. It is cost-effective for all parties involved to settle a case rather than go to trial. Even the Courts require parties to participate in mandatory settlement conferences before going to trial.

There are some cases that are complex, complicated and can only be resolved by going to trial. The Michael Jackson case, however, was not one of these. This case only involved one child making the accusation of child molestation, and the only thing this father wanted was money. Settling this case allowed Michael Jackson the opportunity to put an end to this horrible nightmare that had caused him a great deal of grief, pain, suffering and humiliation. It also meant that his personal life would not be aired before millions of people across the world, any more than already had been done. Settling allowed him to be free, to move on with his life and put the entire matter behind him.

Part 5
Legally Speaking

5.1
The Civil Lawsuit

A civil proceeding is any proceeding other than a criminal proceeding.

Many rumors circulated after the civil lawsuit was settled — that Michael Jackson had bought his way out of a criminal indictment. The civil lawsuit settlement had nothing to do with the criminal investigation. It is my hope that this chapter will give you a clearer understanding of the civil proceedings surrounding this case and how the settlement had no affect on the outcome of the criminal investigation.

The Civil Complaint

Dr. Chandler hired Mr. Feldman, who was a top civil attorney and had served as the head of the Los Angeles Trial Lawyers Association. On September 14, 1993, Feldman filed a thirty million dollar lawsuit in the Los Angeles Superior Court, Santa Monica branch, against Michael Jackson for:

1.) sexual battery; 2.) battery; 3.) seduction; 4.) willful misconduct; 5.) intentional infliction of emotional distress; 6.) fraud; and 7.) negligence. The complaint showed (the 13-year old boy), a minor, by and through his Guardians Ad Litem E. Chandler and J. Chandler as plaintiffs, against the defendant Michael Jackson.

The cause of action speaks for itself. However, the complaint was graphic in its detailed description of the acts which it alleged that Michael Jackson committed against the minor. The complaint alleged that said acts occurred in the county of

Los Angeles, the State of California, and in other locations both within and without the State of California. The complaint also alleged that Michael Jackson repeatedly committed sexual battery upon the minor. The alleged damage caused to the minor was described as: injury to his health, strength and activity, injury to his body and shock and injury to his nervous system; all of which injuries have caused and continue to cause plaintiff great mental, physical and nervous pain and suffering and emotional distress.

The complaint further alleged that the gifts, vacations and trips that Michael Jackson lavished upon the minor was his way of forcing the minor to comply with said sexual demands and to seduce said minor. Although Michael Jackson had lavished many minors and traveling buddies with gifts, trips and toys, none of whom corroborated the 13-year old boy's claim of sexual molestation.

The filing of the civil lawsuit was made while the criminal investigation was still ongoing. Generally, the civil lawsuit is not initiated until after the criminal case has been resolved. The civil lawsuit allows hearsay and circumstantial evidence to be admitted, while the criminal case does not. Therefore, the premature filing of a civil lawsuit while the criminal investigation is ongoing can cause the defendant to be prejudiced or suffer self-incrimination if they are indicted in a criminal case.

Answer to the Complaint

Mr. Fields' office filed the answer to the complaint on October 29, 1993. As soon as the complaint is filed and the defendant answers the complaint, they are entitled to start the discovery phase of the action. The discovery stage allows each party to ask questions, called: Depositions, of the parties or witnesses in a case, request documents (Request for Production of Documents), admit to certain facts (Request for Admissions) and request answers to standard questions called Form Interrogatories. The courts have a limit on the number of interrogatories or documents that can be requested, but through obtaining an order from the court they can exceed that limit. Also, a party can file a protective order blocking or limiting the requests, or limiting the information requested.

Motion to Stay Discovery and Trial
Concurrent with filing the answer to the complaint, Fields' office also filed a Motion for Stay of Discovery and Trial until the statute of limitations expired on the criminal investigation involving the same charges. The statute of limitations for this type of case is six years. A motion is a vehicle by which you can address the court within a short period of time (generally 14 to 28 days) to get an order on a particular issue. The motion was set for a hearing on November 19, 1993 at 1:30 P.M..

In Mr. Fields' Memorandum of Points and Authorities (this is the section of the motion that states the law as it applies to this case, or as it was applied in similar cases before), he alleged that, "the allegations arose solely out of an attempt by Dr. Chandler, the little boy's father, and his father's attorney, Barry Rothman, to extort twenty million dollars from Michael Jackson." He further stated that, "when the defendant refused to pay blackmail money, Dr. Chandler induced his son to make the false allegations of sexual abuse against Michael Jackson."

Mr. Fields' stated reason for filing the Motion to Stay Discovery and Trial was on the grounds that when a civil defendant faces possibility of criminal prosecution for the same factual allegations as alleged in the civil action, according to Federal and California law, the defendant is entitled to Stay the Discovery and Trial in civil proceedings until the statute of limitation has expired on the criminal case. The law that Mr. Fields cited was, Pacers, Inc. v. Superior Court, 162 Cal.App.3d 686, 208 Cal.Rptr. 743 (1984).

Excerpts from Pacers Inc. v. Superior Court reads as follows:
"An order to Stay Discovery until expiration would allow plaintiffs to prepare their lawsuit while alleviating civil defen-

dants from the difficult choice between defending the civil or criminal case."

In Pacer, Inc. v. Superior Court, the defendants refused to answer questions on their deposition based on the fact of possible criminal prosecution. Because of their refusal to answer the deposition questions, the Superior Court granted an order prohibiting defendants from testifying at trial. The Court of Appeals reversed said order and reasoned that the prosecution should not be able to obtain, through civil proceedings, information to which it was not entitled under the criminal discovery rules. Here, although the defendants were not criminal defendants, they were threatened with criminal prosecution, just like in this case. Pacers Inc. v. Superior Court further stated that to allow prosecutors to monitor the civil proceedings to obtain incriminating testimony from defendants through the civil proceedings, "would undermine the Fifth Amendment privilege and violate concepts of fundamental fairness."

The Fifth Amendment states that:
No person shall be held to answer for a capital, or otherwise infamous crime, unless on a presentment or indictment of a Grand Jury, except in cases arising in the land or naval forces, or in the Militia, when in actual service in time of War or public danger; nor shall any person be subject for the same offense to be twice put in jeopardy of life or limb; nor shall be compelled in any criminal case to be a witness against himself, nor be deprived of life, liberty, or property, without due process of law; nor shall private property be taken for public use, without just compensation.

The Federal case held that, "when both criminal and civil proceedings arise out of the same or related transactions, the defendant is entitled to a Stay of Discovery and trial in the civil action until the criminal matter has been fully resolved." Cases cited: Campbell v. Eastland, 307 F.2d 478, cert. denied, 371 U.S. 955, 83 S.Ct. 502, 9 L.Ed. 2d 502 (5th Cir. 1962); Perez v. McQuire 36 F.R.D. 272 (S.D.N.Y. 1964); Paul Harringan &

Sons, Inc. v. Enterprise Animal Oil Co., Inc. 14 F.R.D. 333 (E.D. Pa. 1953).

Fields also cited further cases to support his Motion for Stay as follows: Dustin W. Brown v. The Superior Court. This case asserted a privilege against self-incrimination of the U.S. Constitution, Fifth Amendment. The Court held that privilege was available to defendants even in a civil action.

Dwyer v. Crocker National Bank. This case invoked its privilege against self-incrimination at deposition and refusal to produce documents. The Court of Appeals affirmed that the trial court properly precluded plaintiff from using the self-incrimination privilege as a shield and as a sword.

Patterson v. White, 551 So. 2d 923; 1989 Ala. This case asserted that the discovery request violated his privilege against self-incrimination. White filed answers and raised Fifth Amendment privilege as incriminating. In a Petition for Writ of Mandamus, he argues that his constitutional protection against self-incrimination cannot be waived merely by failing to file objections or responses to civil interrogatories within the time allowed. He maintains that by responding, he waives the privilege. The test for waiver is, "the failure to make a timely objection to the interrogatories or request for production did not constitute a waiver of the constitutional privilege against self-incrimination." The Supreme Judicial Court of Maine ruled in Huot v. Gendron, 284 A.2d 899, 901 (Me. 1971), that, "failure to file timely objections does not constitute a waiver of the privilege against self-incrimination."

The Depositions

Mr. Feldman's office wasted no time in noticing the deposition of Michael Jackson, knowing full well that Michael Jackson was on tour out of the country. Depositions are filed on the attorney representing a party to the action, therefore, even though Michael Jackson was out of the country, it was his attorney's job to make sure he attended the deposition (or reschedule to a date mutually agreeable to all parties concerned). If, however, the parties fail or refuse to attend the noticed deposition, they are allowed to motion the Court for assistance in getting an order for their attendance by way of a Motion to Compel.

Mr. Feldman's office noticed the depositions of Michael Jackson and 11 nonparty witnesses as follows: custodian of records of Pellicano Investigations, custodian of records of Anthony Pellicano, Phillip Le Marque, Stella Le Marque, Gary Hearne, Janelle Wahl, Gayle Goforth, Evangilcan Aquilizor, Anthony Pellicano, LaToya Jackson, Bianca Francia. Michael Jackson's attorneys noticed the depositions of: Plaintiff, the little boy, Barry Rothman, June Schwartz (Chandler) and David Schwartz.

Mr. Feldman's office requested discovery from Michael Jackson as follows: Form Interrogatories, First Set of Special Interrogatories, First Set of Request for Production of Documents, Second Set of Request for Production of Documents and Second Set of Special Interrogatories.

Michael Jackson's attorneys did not refuse to produce him for his deposition, but kept putting the date off. They did finally pinpoint a date to produce Michael Jackson for his deposition sometime in January, but stated that the January date was the soonest he could be produced because of his being out of the country on tour. Mr. Feldman's office was so anxious to take Michael Jackson's deposition that they were even willing to travel out of the country at a mutually agreeable location just to take his deposition earlier than January.

<u>Motion to Compel Michael Jackson's Deposition</u>
While Mr. Fields office was trying to get a Stay of Discovery and the trial date, Mr. Feldman's office, on the other hand, filed a motion to compel Michael Jackson's deposition and to produce documents for inspection. Mr. Feldman was having a hard time deposing Michael Jackson. Michael Jackson and his attorneys responded to all of the requests for inspection of documents by asserting his Fifth Amendment rights.

Mr. Fields' stated his reason for objecting to Mr. Feldman's motion to compel was based on the fact that it impaired Michael

Jackson's constitutional rights until his treatment for drug dependency was completed. He further objected on the grounds that Michael Jackson's deposition should not be taken until the threatened criminal prosecution is disposed of and until his medical condition has been resolved.

Mr. Feldman stated in his reply that Michael Jackson's continued strategy was delay, delay and more delays. He also stuck to his assertion that the memory of a minor is crucial if the victim is to successfully prosecute an action for child molestation. He further stated that Michael Jackson's drug addiction did not prevent him from giving an 8-10 hour deposition in Mexico City on November 8, 1993 in a copyright infringement case while on tour.

Michael Jackson's attorney, Eve H. Wagner, stated that he could not be deposed because of his drug addiction. She described him as being glassy eyed, that he could hardly stay awake, he had difficulty holding physical objects, slurred speech and was unable to focus on issues.

Michael Jackson's doctor in London, Dr. Beauchamp Colelough, issued a statement on November 20, 1993, validating Michael Jackson's condition. He stated that David Forecast, Michael Jackson's physician in Mexico City, and Miss Elizabeth Taylor brought Michael Jackson to him on November 12, 1993 to participate in a 6 to 8 week program for his dependency to pain killers. It was Dr. Daniel Forecast who recommended that Michael Jackson cancel the remainder of his tour. Mr. Fields spoke with Mr. Forecast over the phone where he informed him that Michael Jackson would be canceling the tour, which would cost him millions of dollars and be put into professional care. He refused to disclose where Michael Jackson would be receiving his treatment because of the media attention it would draw, which would destroy Michael Jackson's possibility of receiving proper care.

The law that Fields cited in his Reply was that there was no constitutional right to a Stay. U.S. v. Kordel, 397 U.S. 1, 90 S. Ct. 763 25 L.Ed.2d 1 (1970); People v. Coleman, 13 Cal.3d. 867 (1975).

Once the right against self-incrimination has been invoked, a Stay is not mandatory but rests within the sound discretion of the Court. Fed. S&L Ins. Corp. v. Molinaro, 889 F.2d 899 (9th Cir. 1989). The Court of Appeals held that the privilege against self-incrimination may be invoked not only by a criminal defendant, but also by parties or witnesses in a civil action. However, while the privilege of a criminal defendant is absolute, in a civil case a witness or party may be required to waive the privilege or accept the civil consequence of silence if he does exercise it. There is a wide range of civil sanctions that may be imposed upon a civil litigant who invokes his or her Fifth Amendment right. Although one cannot be penalized for asserting the privilege against self-incrimination, one is held accountable for the consequences that directly results from its assertions.

Defendant's opposition to the motion to compel argued that his deposition should be continued until the threatened criminal prosecution is disposed of and until defendant's current medical treatment is concluded.

Code of Civil Procedure section 36 is mandatory and requires that preference be given in actions such as the case at hand when plaintiff is under the age of 14 years old.

Motion to Compel Further Responses

Mr. Cochran opposed Mr. Feldman's motion to compel further responses to written discovery stating that "it will violate Michael Jackson's constitutional rights." "That Michael Jackson be given the same right to have his testimony heard for the first time at trial without fear that the prosecution will try to impeach his credibility." Mr. Cochran stated that, "the law enforcement agency has sought and gained access to all discovery in this action." He also opposed the request due to it being overbroad, seeking information not related to plaintiff's claim of sexual molestation, that the information sought was protected by work product and attorney/client privilege, and the request for financial information was premature. He also contended that because of the changed circumstances, Michael

Jackson should not be required to respond to discovery until the conclusion of the pending criminal investigation and that plaintiff should not be permitted to use civil discovery to harass and intimidate third parties.

Motion for Trial Preference

Mr. Feldman hit them with another blow by filing a Motion for Trial Preference. This is a special request to have the trial heard within 120 days after the motion is granted. This request is generally given to children under the age of 14 years old and seniors due to their inability to remember details after a prolonged period of time. The Motion for Preference was set to be heard on November 16, 1993, and a trial date of March 16, 1994 was requested.

Mr. Feldman stated in the Trial Preference Motion that the system designed to protect a child from the embarrassment and ridicule of being a victim in this type of crime has totally failed this minor due to the worldwide publicity of the leaked Department of Children's Services report. Mr. Feldman, obviously good at painting pictures of despair, further alleged that a delay in this case would send a message to the world that no child would be safe from someone with a superstar status such as Michael Jackson. He concluded that his client, the 13-year old boy, was entitled to live the remainder of his childhood without a cloud over his head that he was an extortionist and liar. (He was referring to statements Mr. Pellicano made to the press which was televised stating that Dr. Chandler and Mr. Rothman were extortionists and liars). Mr. Pellicano submitted a Declaration to the Court refuting Mr. Feldman's claim and stated that his comments were directed to Dr. Chandler and Mr. Rothman and were never directed at the 13-year old boy.

The law that Mr. Feldman used to base his request for trial preference was Civil Code of Procedure section 36, which requires that a party to a civil action for personal injuries who is under the age of 14 be provided with a speedy trial date within 120 days. Mr. Feldman further stated that his request would allow his client to retreat from the media spotlight and return to a normal life. He contended that his client's efforts to put this case behind him were being stifled by delay tactics and media manipulation by Michael Jackson, his attorneys, investigators and publicists.

The Opposition to Motion for Trial Preference

The Points and Authorities filed by Mr. Fields in opposition to plaintiff's Motion for Trial Preference stated that the Motion for Trial Preference should be denied because Civil Code of Procedure section 36 did not apply in this case. He further stated that trying the case before the disposition of the criminal case would impair Michael Jackson's constitutional rights and would be contrary to case law in this state.

Mr. Feldman was persistent in painting the picture in his pleading that the 13-year old boy was being lured and enticed by Michael Jackson's acts of kindness and by the many gifts and trips that he lavished upon him. Mr. Fields was equally eloquent in stating that the 13-year old boy's conduct in accepting the many gifts and continued friendship with Michael Jackson showed a willingness to engage in the friendship and therefore did not constitute as unlawful consent.

Mr. Feldman filed a declaration by Dr. Evan Chandler in support of the Motion for Trial Preference which had one statement: that the child was under the age of 14. That was it! Dr. Chandler did not state anything else in his declaration, which is a written statement under oath declaring statements of truth. I have never seen a declaration concerning an important case this short in my entire legal career. A declarant will usually attest to several facts, especially concerning an important case like this one. They will also declare that said facts are true and correct and state their willingness to be called to competently testify under penalty of perjury. Is it possible that the information that Dr. Chandler declared was the only information he could competently testify under penalty of perjury?

Mr. Feldman filed a Supplemental Memorandum of Points and Authorities in support of his Motion for Trial Preference just one day before the November 23, 1993 hearing date. He submitted a full legislative history of Section 36 which provided the Court with the basis for plaintiff's claim for preference. It specifically stated that Section 36 was intended to apply to actions such as the present action for sexual battery and related causes of actions because a child's memory is developing and therefore cannot remember like an adult. He also stated that child memories are fragile.

Ex Parte Application for Interim Order to Stay Discovery

Mr. Fields filed an Ex Parte Application for an Interim Order to Stay Plaintiff's Discovery until the Court ruled on defendant's Motion to Stay Discovery and Trial. This move was necessary to prevent the discovery that was propounded by the plaintiffs from being due before the Court made a ruling on defendant's Motion to Stay the Discovery and Trial. The Ex Parte hearing was heard on November 5, 1993, and the Court ordered that all discovery was stayed until the November 23, 1993, hearing on the Motion to Stay Discovery and Trial was to be heard.

Mr. Feldman's opposition to the Ex Parte application was that they would have to reschedule and re-notice the depositions of 11 non-party witnesses and that this was another stall and delay tactic by defendant. In the interim, the Court did order to allow the depositions of Mr. Pellicano, Phillip Le Marque, Stella L. Marque, Gary Hearne, Janelle Wahl, (the 13-year old Chandler boy), Gail Goforth, Evan Chandler, Evangelian Aquilian, Barry Rothman, June Schwartz, David Schwartz, Anthony Pellicano, La Toya Jackson and Bianca Francia to go forward.

The Outcome of the Court Hearing

On November 23, 1993, the Court heard the Motion for Trial Preference, the Motion to Stay Trial and Discovery, the Motion to Compel the Deposition of Michael Jackson, and Defendant's Request for Stay of Ruling. The Court ruled as follows:

(Chandler) Motion for Trial Preference..... *Granted*

(M. Jackson) Motion to Compel Deposition..... *Denied w/o Prejudice*

(Chandler) Motion to Compel Mr. Jackson's Depo..... *Granted*

(M. Jackson) Request to Stay Ruling..... *Denied*

Michael Jackson lost all four motions. It was obvious from a legal standpoint of view that the scales of justice were not pointing in Michael Jackson's favor. Instead, it was weighing heavily in favor of the 13-year old boy. Michael Jackson's attorneys were applying precedent laws which were applied in a similar sexual battery case. Pacers Inc. v. Superior Court specifically held that it is improper invasion of the defendant's constitutional rights not to stay civil proceedings where a criminal investigation is ongoing. But Mr. Feldman's trump card was, "a child's memory is developing," and their inability to, "remember like an adult." This law was designed to protect a small child's ability to recall for prolonged periods of time after being a victim and/or witness to a crime. This case, however, involved a 13-year old boy, who was soon to be turning 14 years old.

<u>Johnnie Cochran Joins the Legal Team</u>
Immediately after Michael Jackson's team of attorneys lost crucial motions that would have given him a chance to win this lawsuit, Johnnie Cochran Jr. associated in as counsel on December 13, 1993. Johnnie Cochran wasted no time in filing a Motion for Protective Order, prohibiting the parties and their attorneys and agents from disclosing the information obtained through discovery in this case to anyone other than the parties and their attorneys and authorized representatives. Mr. Cochran stated that a protective order was necessary to protect:

1.) Michael Jackson's right to privacy and undue embarrassment and annoyance; 2.) his right to receive a fair trial; and 3.) the rights of witnesses from undue embarrassment and annoyance.

In Mr. Cochran's motion he further stated that if the protective order was not granted, Michael Jackson would require a Stay of the Civil action because of the law enforcement's expressed intent to use the Civil Discovery as part of it's investigation. Mr. Cochran asserted that the law enforcement agency was delaying their investigation in order to gain information elicited through their discovery efforts. This is precisely the reason why Mr. Feldman tried to obtain a Stay of Discovery and Trial to prevent information obtained in the civil lawsuit from being used in the criminal investigation.

The introduction of Mr. Cochran's motion for a protective order pleaded that the release of information by plaintiff's attorney would undermine Michael Jackson's right and deprive him of a fair trial. Mr. Cochran eloquently pointed out that the protective order was not only needed for Michael Jackson's best interest, but was also necessary to protect the lives of witnesses. He wanted no party to disclose any information revealed through discovery to media or law enforcement.

Mr. Cochran also stated that the protective order was necessary to not only protect the privacy of the 13-year old minor, but the privacy of other children involved in the case. Originally, the attorneys came to a mutual agreement not to reveal anything to the media concerning the case. Mr. Feldman repudiated the agreement stating that he could no longer honor any agreement regarding publicity because of Michael Jackson's family declaring his innocence.

The Code that Mr. Cochran used to base his legal position was Code of Civil Procedure section 2025(i) which states that: the Court, for good cause, may invoke any order that justice requires to protect any party, deponent, or other from annoyance, embarrassment, or oppression. Also, section 2017(c) applies to general discovery; section 2031(e) applies to document production and section 2033(e) applies to request for admission.

Mr. Cochran further cited that a protective order was necessary to protect third parties' privacy rights and litigants from unwarranted annoyance or embarrassment. Boler v. S. Ct. Of Solano County, 201 Cal.App.3d 467, 475, 247 Cal.Rptr. 185 (1987). The trial court has discretion to order that information obtained through discovery not be disclosed and be filed under seal as confidential. Coalition Against Police Abuse v. S.Ct., 170 Cal.App.3d 888, 216 Cal.Rptr. 614 (1985).

Because of the lurid allegations against Michael Jackson, Mr. Cochran felt that the questions asked of the minors and their parents would be highly embarrassing, personal and private. He also felt that because of the running commentary by plaintiff's attorney on information gathered during the discovery had and would add to the media frenzy and exacerbate the massive invasion of privacy of Michael Jackson's life. Especially concerning information pertaining to his residence, routines, habits and security being revealed and public disclosure would violate Michael Jackson's right to privacy.

The California Constitution, Article I, section 16, says that: "A defendant is entitled to a fair civil trial by an impartial jury." Dorshkind v. Harry N. Koff Agency, Inc., 64 Cal.App.3d, 302, 308, 134 Cal.Rptr. 344 (1976). Mr. Cochran stated that the media circus has already prevented Michael Jackson from the right to a fair trial and that the protective order would minimize evidence from being spread all over the world by plaintiff's attorney.

The District Attorney's office had threatened to subpoena the discovery taken in the civil lawsuit to use in their criminal investigation. Mr. Cochran's position was that discovery should not be a tool to further the District Attorney's investigation. The protective order, in his estimation, would prevent information revealed through discovery to be used in aid of the pending investigation of the same charges by law enforcement which would give the state an unfair advantage. The District Attorney's office did, in fact, ask the plaintiff's attorneys for a copy of the deposition transcript after the deposition was taken in the civil action. When the plaintiff's attorney refused to provide a copy of the deposition, a Deputy District Attorney informed Mr. Feldman that, "they could serve him with a search warrant if necessary."

In Pacers Inc. v. Superior Court, it further states that, "the prosecution should not be able to obtain, through the medium of the civil proceedings, information to which it was not entitled under the Criminal Discovery rules..." Discovery is presumed to be private. It is taken behind closed doors in the presence of a Certified Court Reporter in the presence of only the party being deposed, the attorneys and sometimes a third party mediator. The transcript is not ordinarily lodged with the Court except in cases of appeal, motions or when it is used as an exhibit. The interrogatories, responses, production of documents and admissions are also not filed with the court except for the same reasons. Mr. Cochran's point was that the media had no greater right under the First Amendment to access information revealed through the Civil Discovery than private citizens.

Mr. Feldman agreed to the entry of a stipulated protective order, but took exception to being able to respond to false allegations and to providing information to law enforcement agencies.

Opposition to Protective Order by the Times Mirror Company

The Times Mirror Company, the publisher of the L.A. Times, filed an opposition to the motion for protective order, contesting the order restricted public access to any Court proceedings, including the Discovery conducted. It's position was that the media had a right to intervene in ongoing civil and criminal actions to raise their objection to a protective order to seek access. Public Citizen v. Liggett Group, Inc., 858 F2d, 775, 783_84 (1st Cir. 1988), cert denied, 488 U.S. 1030 (1989).

It further stated that the headliners of major news organizations throughout the world had focused on the investigation of child molestation charges against Michael Jackson and that the public interest and attention were riveted on the allegations. It also stated that Michael Jackson and the public investigator took advantage of the media to issue numerous statements to the public and that now, because he didn't want negative publicity, he sought a blanket closure order. It requested that the Court deny Michael Jackson's motion and permit the public access to information about this matter which was of great public interest.

It contended even further that gag orders are granted only for *good cause* and none has been shown in this case. It also stated that Mr. Cochran's contentions regarding the defendant's right to a fair trial were harmed by pretrial publicity, invasion of privacy, and that Mr. Cochran's position concerning third party witnesses being in danger and hounded and government taking advantage of civil information in criminal proceedings was baseless. In essence, the Times Mirror said that Michael Jackson's attorneys had not shown good cause to assert First Amendment concerns. The U.S. Supreme Court recognized that pretrial protective orders are subject to scrutiny under the First Amendment, and must be made within Rule 26(c) which requires a showing of good faith. It also stated that there is a presumptive right to discovery materials. Public Citizen v. Leggett, supra.

Federal Rule of Civil Procedure 26(c) states: Upon a motion by the party or by the person from whom discovery is being sought, for good cause, may make any order which justice requires to protect a party from annoyance, embarrassment, oppression, or undue burden or expense. The Times Mirror disagreed with Mr. Cochran's statement that publicity would prevent Michael Jackson from receiving a fair trial.

The Times Mirror continued by stating that there are 2,900,000 possible jurors in Los Angeles County which are pulled from the records of the Department of Motor Vehicle's database. A protective order, in its opinion, would keep reliable information from the public while allowing unreliable information to be reported, and that Michael Jackson did not have a right to be free of adverse publicity. There was no invasion of privacy where the facts at issue are already known. Sipper v. Chronicle Publishing, 154 Cal.App.3d 1040, 1047, 201 Cal.Rptr. 665 (1984).

The Time Mirror further stated that in order to state an invasion of privacy claim, it must also be proven that the facts revealed were so offensive as to shock the community's notion of decency. Briscoe v. Reader's Digest Assn. Inc., 4 Cal.3d 529, 541, 93 Cal.Rptr. 866 (1971).

The People's (Garcetti and Sneddon) Response to Defendant's Motion for Protective Order

Gil Garcetti and Thomas Sneddon, the District Attorneys from Los Angeles and Santa Barbara, jointly filed a response to Mr. Cochran's motion for protective order. They wanted to assure the Court that the progress of the child molestation investigation of Michael Jackson was not connected to, or dictated by, the discovery process in the civil case. They stated that they had no intention to slow or delay their investigation for the purpose of obtaining information derived during the Civil Discovery. They also confirmed that they had no intention to disclose any information they obtained during the course of their investigation to anyone who was not in the law enforcement agency.

However, they felt strongly that they were entitled to obtain all depositions, statements, and any documentary or derivative information from any witness who had evidence relating to their criminal investigation. Therefore, they required access to all Civil Discovery because serious injuries deserve to be fully investigated. Their position was that the law enforcement agency should not be precluded or restricted from gathering any information which pertains to investigation which is not privileged. They also addressed the fact that three days before filing their papers, Michael Jackson's attorneys requested an opportunity to present evidence which might impact their filing decision. They stated, "how can they now argue fundamental fairness?" With boldness, they contended that there is no authority which prohibits law enforcement access to Civil Discovery.

Mr. Garcetti and Mr. Sneddon further stated that the case which Mr. Cochran relied on, Pacers Inc. v. Superior Court, was decided before the passage of Proposition 115, California Constitution, Article I, Section 28(d), which prohibits the exclusion of relevant evidence in a criminal proceeding and Section 30(c) requires reciprocal discovery. Under Proposition 115, only Fifth Amendment self-incrimination discovery remains protected. In decisions upholding Proposition 115, both legislative and judicial recognition of strong public policy to promote balance and fairness in our Criminal Justice System and to remove roadblocks which hinder the ascertainment of the truth. In essence, the criminal investigation should be unimpeded.

They contended that a search warrant may be issued when: "The property or things to be seized consist of any item or constitutes any evidence which tends to show a felony has been committed or tends to show that a particular person has committed a felony." Penal Code 1524(a)(4). Subpoenas may be issued for: "Those witnesses whose testimony, in his opinion, is material in an investigation before the Grand Jury." Penal Code 939.2.

They said that *privacy rights* must yield to a criminal investigation. Absent violation of the Fourth Amendment privacy rights cannot be justification for preventing the state from investigating criminal activity where there is probable cause. Although Mr. Cochran did not make this point, they also stated that, "fear of getting caught," was not a privacy right. In case criminal charges are filed, and whatever is filed or introduced or said in court then becomes a matter of public records.

Opposition to Protective Order by Radio & Television News Assn.

An opposition to Mr. Cochran's motion for protective order was filed by the Radio & Television News Assn. Of Southern California. Its position was the same as the others that opposed the protective order. Their position was that the protective order pertaining to pretrial discovery implicated the First Amendment and was disfavorable and, where issued, should be drawn as narrow as possible. It stated that the invasion of privacy theory presented by Mr. Cochran was hollow in this case because public interest of the best known public figure in the world is unavoidable.

The Outcome of the Motion for Protective Order

The hearing on the Motion for Protective order was heard on December 17, 1993. The Court ruled as follows:

1.) The motion to prevent parties-in-action from disclosing informal and formal discovery material to the District Attorney's office was denied.

2.) The Stipulation of counsel ordered as follows:
Neither side shall release to media or persons not a party to the litigation a) videotapes; b) Discovery; c) information regarding personal security of Michael Jackson; or medical or psychiatric records.

3.) The motion to compel be filed under seal.

4.) The motion to compel further responses to written discovery was denied.

In this decision, the Court did not completely rule against Michael Jackson. It did take some of Mr. Cochran's points concerning privacy in ordering that the motions to compel be filed under seal and by denying the motion to compel further responses to discovery. However, Mr. Cochran's main interest was the protective order and keeping the District Attorney's office from accessing formal and informal discovery material obtained in the civil lawsuit, which was denied. The Court's decision, in essence, favored the District Attorney's office giving them free reign to access and obtain any and all information that was produced in discovery in the civil lawsuit.

Mr. Cochran's repeated reason for making this request was not to impede the criminal investigation nor to prevent the district attorney's office from accessing the information disclosed in discovery, but to protect Michael Jackson's right to privacy as well as the privacy of the children involved in the case and their families. This issue was probably crucial to Michael Jackson, personally, because he always valued his privacy. His life was never an open book and he allowed very few people access to his private life.

The stipulation between counsel, which stated that neither side would release videotapes, discovery information, information regarding Michael Jackson's personal security and medical or psychiatric records to the media or persons not a party to the litigation, did help to control the flow of confidential information from getting into the hands of the press/media. It did not block the press and public's ability to gain access to information concerning the lawsuit as it was unfolding.

Although the District Attorney's office argument was the strongest in stating that not only the constitutional laws but also legislative laws were written to prevent any type of obstruction of justice, they still never succeeded in indicting Michael Jackson on the criminal charges. Their presence and vocal opposition weighed heavily in the civil proceeding, but still took no effect in the filing of a criminal charge.

It is my opinion, that the District Attorney's office proved why the Court's decision, in Pacers Inc. v. Superior Court, should have applied to Michael Jackson's case and should have prevailed. The Court held in Pacers Inc. v. Superior Court that the defendant was entitled to a Stay of Discovery in the civil action until the criminal statute of limitations ran to preserve the defendant's constitutional rights, and that it would be fundamentally unfair for the prosecution to take advantage of the Civil Discovery to obtain information about the defendant's case which it could not obtain through Criminal Discovery. The Court recognized, in Pacers Inc. v. Superior Court, that a Stay would cause delay and inconvenience to the plaintiff but that protecting a party's constitutional rights is paramount.

California law mandates a Stay of Civil proceedings pending the final outcome of the criminal case when a civil trial takes place while a criminal charge on the same facts is under consideration. Not granting the defendant the protection under the constitution, they are sacrificing their right to due process in the civil action as well as their right to avoid self-incrimination in the criminal proceeding.

In Dwyer v. Crocker National Bank, 194 Cal.App.3d 1418, 1432 (1987), it cites Pacers Inc. v. Superior Court, as well, and implies that where the Stay Motion is brought by a defendant, Pacers Inc. v. Superior Court correctly states the California law.

The Stay rule has been repeatedly followed in other jurisdictions such as U.S. v. Certain Real Property, 751 F.Supp. 1060, 1063_1064 (E.D.N.Y. 1989); Paul Harrigan & Sons, Inc. v. Enterprise Animal Oil Co., 14 F.R.D. 333, 335 (E.D. Pa. 1953) and in Peden v. U.S., 512 F.2d F.2d 1099, 1103 (Ct. Cl. 1975) It was believed to have been the practice to *freeze* civil proceedings when a criminal prosecution involving the same facts was warming up or underway.

The District Court in Harrigan also ruled that while a Stay will undoubtedly cause inconvenience and delay to the plaintiff, protection of the defendants' constitutional rights is the more important consideration.

Even the Supreme Court of Alabama ordered a Stay of the civil proceedings, ruling that the defendant must not be forced to choose between a constitutional right and a potential loss in a state matter. Weighing the defendant's interest in postponing the civil actions against the prejudice that might result to the plaintiffs because of the delay, compels a postponement. It also stated that a defendant facing civil proceedings and criminal prosecution denies him due process.

Because of the Court rulings, Michael Jackson was at a disadvantage in having to prepare for trial within 120 days in a case that involved massive witnesses. The police had seized all of his personal records and would not provide copies nor even a list of what they took. The District Attorney's office was operating, with the blessings of the Court, in violation of Michael Jackson's constitutional rights, and the Court was weighing heavily in favor of the 13-year old boy.

I have one question to ask you, the reader, now that you have more information concerning what was going on in the legal realm: What would you have done at this point with these same factors weighing out of your favor? Would you have continued with the litigation or settled the case as Michael Jackson chose to do?

There were numerous other lawsuits that stemmed from the child molestation lawsuit. There were multiple lawsuits which involved the parties to this action against other involved parties. Everyone was going lawsuit crazy. Some of the lawsuits that stemmed from this action, were as follows:

Evan Chandler v. June Chandler Schwartz and David Schwartz.

Dr. Evan Chandler filed a lawsuit against June and David Schwartz in August of 1994, for invasion of privacy, violation of Penal Code section 632; intentional infliction of emotional distress and conspiracy.

Dr. Chandler stated in the Complaint that in June of 1993, he noticed a change in his son's personality, mental and physical well being. He further stated that David Schwartz recorded their telephone conversation and gave the recordings to a third party with the intent to publish said recordings and that on August 31, 1993, the recordings were published and disseminated to the news media throughout the world.

June Schwartz answered the complaint by asserting that the action was brought in bad faith, without probable cause and in an attempt to avoid payment of past due child support. She further asserted that said action was being brought to promote his own hope for celebrity status and a cruel plan to gain control over the assets of the parties' minor child by manipulating the child's affection.

June Schwartz further stated in her affirmative defenses that the complaint was barred by virtue of the *Release of Claims* executed by plaintiff as of July 30, 1993, and pursuant to a confidentially sealed release agreement between plaintiff, defendant and a third party. Because the plaintiff was not the victim of the sexual abuse and did not witness such events, the plaintiff lacked standing to pursue his cause of action, and that the injuries were the proximate cause of plaintiff's own negligence, carelessness and/or other legal fault. The Complaint is based on allegations that the defendant improperly cared for and/or failed to protect the plaintiff's minor child from sexual abuse and that the defendant was unaware of the abuse, and as the child's custodial parent, her conduct was privileged. The plaintiff owed her back child support payments in the sum of seventy thousand dollars.

David Schwartz cross complained against Dr. Chandler for invasion of privacy, violation of Penal Code 632, and intentional infliction of emotional distress. In his statement of facts Mr. Schwartz contended that in the summer of 1993, the Schwartz family was torn apart by Michael Jackson's interference in the family. Schwartz further stated that he did not think Michael Jackson had molested his stepson.

Mr. Schwartz stated that on July 7, 1993, he received a call from Dr. Chandler wherein he was abusive, belligerent and violent. He stated that it was not uncommon for Dr. Chandler to become violent. Mr. Schwartz said the reason he recorded his conversation with Dr. Chandler was because Dr. Chandler told him he had thoughts of killing the entire family, including the children, and that Mr. Schwartz recorded the conversation out of fear concerning Dr. Chandler's threats to kill the family, including Mr. Schwartz.

Mr. Schwartz further stated that the reason he presented the recordings to Mr. Pellicano and Mr. Fields was to enlist their aide in protecting his family and that it would prove that Dr. Chandler had threatened violence. He said Mr. Fields and Mr. Pellicano did not return the recordings, nor were they able to assist him. Mr. Schwartz alleged that Mr. Pellicano gave the recordings to Mary Fisher, without his permission, who used some of the contents of the tape for the article she wrote entitled, *Was Michael Jackson Framed?*, which was published by Gentleman's Quarterly in 1994.

Mary Fisher was subpoenaed in this case to produce information concerning the article, *Was Michael Jackson Framed?*. Mary's attorneys claimed the First Amendment right which states that as a reporter, she: "...cannot be compelled to disclose unpublished information obtained in gathering information for dissemination to the public." Her attorneys requested that the subpoena be quashed or limited. The Court allowed the subpoena to be quashed as it pertained to the *unpublished* articles only.

The case was dismissed with prejudice.

Schwartz v. Chandler

David Schwartz filed a lawsuit against Dr. Chandler for damages—for brain damage, two counts for assault, and two counts for battery.

Mr. Schwartz asserted that on July 9, 1993, at Dr. Chandler's house in Brentwood, Dr. Chandler approached him in a menacing manner with a closed fist and threatened to strike him with his hands and feet. He stated that Dr. Chandler wrestled him to the ground and began to kick him and spat on him.

Mr. Schwartz further asserted that once again while at Mr. Feldman's office in August of 1993, there was another altercation in which Dr. Chandler punched Mr. Schwartz in his temple, causing him to lose consciousness.

June Schwartz filed a Declaration in support of her husband, Mr. Schwartz and asserted that the Department of Children's Services interviewed the 13-year old boy in their home. She further stated that since the news of the child molestation had been broadcast worldwide, they had been the victims of people stalking their home, as well as threats and bizarre phone calls from Michael Jackson's fans. She also stated that her son had suffered physical threats, photos had been taken of them and distributed worldwide, and that one of Michael Jackson's fans broke into their home.

This case was dismissed on January 29, 1996.

5.2
The Criminal Investigation

The criminal investigation being spearheaded by Mr. Sneddon of the Santa Barbara County and Mr. Garcetti of Los Angeles County, was totally different from the civil proceeding. This was one of the most vigorously sought after criminal indictments ever pursued in a joint effort by two counties.

The Fifth Amendment to the U.S. Constitution and Article I, section 15 of the California Constitution gives the defendant, in a criminal case, the option of testifying or refraining from doing so. The option to testify or not to is one of the most important rights provided by the constitution, and the decision to testify is one of the most important decisions that a defendant must face in a criminal proceeding.

In Mr. Garcetti and Mr. Sneddon's opposition to Michael Jackson's attorney's Motion for a Protective Order in December of 1993, they asserted that they wanted to assure the Court that, "the progress of the child molestation investigation of Michael Jackson was not connected to or dictated by the discovery process in the civil case." They openly and publicly declared that the civil case had nothing whatsoever to do with the criminal case. It was their intention to take full advantage of the information obtained in the civil proceedings to assist their efforts in the criminal prosecution, however, even with that assurance they were still unable to collectively indict Michael Jackson on the child molestation allegations.

More than 400 witnesses were interviewed, two Grand Juries were impaneled, and tens of thousands of taxpayer dollars were spent over an eight month period before Mr. Garcetti and Mr. Sneddon decided to end their criminal investigation. Mr. Garcetti announced that the investigation would remain open pending any witnesses coming forward until the six year statute of limitation had expired.

Had Mr. Sneddon and Mr. Garcetti found anything credible to indict Michael Jackson on, he would have been indicted and tried on the criminal charges. The settlement of the civil proceedings did not interfere with the criminal prosecution case nor did Michael Jackson buy his way out of being indicted. The only problem the settlement caused, was that under California law children cannot be forced to testify against their will, but the law does not allow authorities to punish victims of sex crimes who decline to testify. The reason why they could not indict was because the 13-year old boy was their only witness, and without his cooperation they had no case.

Two Grand Juries, which consisted of 24 peers in two different counties, an extensive search of Michael Jackson's Neverland Ranch, Century City condo, his parent's Encino home, and even Michael Jackson's body search, interviews with over 200 men, women, boys and girls, and even traveling out of the country to interview witnesses, did not produce any evidence to support a criminal indictment for child molestation.

Criminal cases deal primarily with the issue of guilt or innocence and a jury must come to an unanimous decision that a crime was committed beyond a reasonable doubt. The outcome in a criminal proceeding, if a party is found guilty, is primarily about punishment, and/or fines, or both. This differs from the civil proceeding... which is about money.

Although civil and criminal cases are distinctly different areas of law and play by a different set of rules, as mentioned previously, an individual can be charged in both venues. The criminal case is usually tried first, and once a determination of guilt has been established, the harmed party files a civil lawsuit to collect damages for said crime.

— REDEMPTION —

In the O.J. Simpson murder trial, we saw that after he was acquitted in the murder case he was, in essence, tried again in the civil lawsuit and was found liable for the deaths of Nicole Simpson and Ron Goldman. O.J.'s case was different because he was acquitted of the criminal charge and tried again on the civil charge. He was tried twice for the same crime, irrespective of the *double jeopardy* rule, that says you cannot be tried twice for the same crime.

In Michael Jackson's case, so much energy was directed towards indicting him on the child molestation allegation that the extortion investigation received minimum attention and investigation. Some people call it black justice in white America. There was a time in America when a serious crime was only a crime if it was committed by someone black. That same crime committed by someone white would always end in a lesser punishment or in an acquittal. This included murder, rape, robbery, stealing people's land and even police brutality. There is no doubt that this practice caused a lot of anxiety in many Americans, especially in the black community. But this case also involved the word of a 13-year old white boy against an adult black male, totally denying Michael Jackson's constitutional rights as well as ignoring proven state and federal laws that applied to other cases.

5.3
Attorney / Client Privilege

This chapter will give the public a better understanding of what attorney/client privilege is, the reason for it, and why it was created. It will also explain what breaches the privilege between the attorney, and client and further explain why all communications between attorney and client are not privileged and how that privilege is lost.

An attorney is identified as: a person authorized, or reasonably believed by the client to be authorized to practice law in any state or nation. Evid Code section 950. Client means: a person who, directly or through an authorized representative, consults a lawyer for the purpose of retaining the lawyer or securing legal services or advice from him in his professional capacity.... Evidence Code section 951.

The attorney/client privilege was created in the eighteenth and nineteenth century for the purpose of protecting communications between the attorney and client, and client secrets. It allowed such communications to be kept in confidence so that the attorney could give reasonably informed professional advice. The assumption for the privilege is that the client will be more open and honest with the lawyer if it is known that their communication cannot be used against them. Also, the more open and honest the client is with the lawyer concerning all the facts, the lawyer can better assist in offering legal advice. This allows the client to communicate to his lawyer in confidence. The lawyer must take all steps necessary to maintain that confidence.

— REDEMPTION —

The essence of attorney/client privilege is to protect a client's right to seek and secure legal representation for ethical business dealings. Even if a client seeks legal representation for ethical reasons, and the attorney later learns of unethical dealings on the part of his client, he is still covered under the attorney client privilege. (Note: Not everything conveyed by a client to an attorney is immune from compelled disclosure in civil litigation or from a Grand Jury subpoena in the criminal context.) There are many communications that clients and attorneys would like to believe are privileged, and in fact are not.

The privilege, however, does not protect all communications under an attorneys control. Compelled disclosure in litigation happens more frequently than many people realize. It is an attorney's duty to know the parameters of the privilege and protect what would otherwise have to be disclosed. A skilled lawyer, though, can uncover communications that were meant to be hidden.

The rule that places the seal of secrecy on communications between client and attorney is the necessity, in the interest and administration of justice, of the aid of persons having knowledge of the law and skilled in its practice, which assistance can only be safely and readily availed of when free from the consequences or the apprehension of disclosure. Hunt v. Blackburn, 128 U.S. 464, 470 (1888).

The protection granted to the attorney/client relationship is based upon the assumption that lawyers are consulted for the purpose of ethical and legal activity, rather than to devise means to break the law. When the fundamental trust that society places in lawyers is breached so, too, is the protection that the attorney/client privilege affords. The attorney-client privilege was designed to facilitate the administration of justice, not to thwart it.

The focus of the exception is on the client's intentions when legal counsel was sought. In other words, what was his motive for seeking legal representation. Was it for bonafide legal reasons? Or were his intentions fraudulent?

The crime/fraud waiver is based on the recognition that when the client seeks an attorney's assistance to commit a crime or fraud, the privilege serves no useful purpose and its protection should be withdrawn. This rule is true whether or not the lawyer was aware of the client's unlawful goal.

Although a client's state of mind in seeking legal representation is difficult to prove, the appellate courts have imposed a stringent limitation on the use of conduct evidence in determining whether to apply the crime/fraud exception. (Definition: Conduct — the act, manner, or process of carrying on; personal behavior.)

Dr. Chandler clearly stated in the recorded conversation with Dave Schwartz, that was aired all over the world, that he, "hired an attorney named Barry K. Rothman because he is DEVIOUS, NASTY and CRUEL, and can destroy everybody in sight." Fraud destroys the attorney/client privilege. The privilege protecting communications between attorney and client is lost if the relation is abused in cases where the client seeks advice that will serve him in the commission of a fraud. Wilson v. Superior Court, 148 Cal.App.2d 433, 433 [307 P.2d 37]; Abbott v. Superior Court, 78 Cal App.2d 19, 21 [177 P.2d 317].

Once fraud is determined, said findings should have ethical implications. It could be argued that a client used a lawyer's representation for fraudulent purposes without the lawyer's knowledge; however, that argument seems highly improbable. The very nature of the abuse suggests that it may have been the idea of the attorney.

California Evidence Code section 956, states: "There is no privilege under this article if the services of the lawyer were sought or obtained to enable or aid anyone to commit or plan to commit a crime or a fraud." (California's Statutory Exceptions to the Principle of Professional Confidentiality)

5.4
Litigation Facts

A very crucial part of understanding the facts surrounding this case involves knowing what was going on in the court system. Litigation means: to institute or subject to legal proceedings.

After Mr. Rothman ceased being Dr. Chandler's attorney, at least on the surface, he filed a lawsuit against Michael Jackson and Anthony Pellicano, claiming that he was forced to withdraw from representing Dr. Chandler because of the defendant's alleged conduct. Mr. Rothman further claimed that defendant interfered with the contract between Dr. Chandler and his son by publicly accusing them of extortion when Mr. Rothman, was in good faith, protecting his clients. I take exception to Mr. Rothman's statement in his complaint based on Dr. Chandler's stated reasons for hiring Mr. Rothman as being the opposite of good faith. Dr. Chandler was crystal clear in stating that he hired Mr. Rothman to, "destroy everybody in sight in any devious, nasty, cruel way that he can do it..."

Mr. Rothman also accused defendants of filing a false police report with the LAPD for extortion, and that said false reporting forced Mr. Rothman from being able to represent his clients because he could not continue under the cloud of such false charges.

Mr. Rothman alleged and asserted that the defendants also drove a wedge between him and the Chandler family. He further contended that Dr. Chandler hired new legal counsel who successfully concluded the claim that he had initiated. Of course, he charged them with slander and libelous statements which he claimed exposed him to hatred, contempt, and ridicule. He claimed to have suffered loss of reputation, shame, mortification, embarrassment and humiliation.

Mr. Rothman was no match for Michael Jackson's new law firm, Katten Machin & Zavis. During the course of his litigation efforts against the defendants, Mr. Rothman made a lot of litigation errors which Michael Jackson's attorneys were quick to point out and correct openly in court. At this time Mr. Rothman was being represented by Wylie A. Aitken. The motion was taken off calendar pursuant to a request of the moving party on November 4, 1993.

Mr. Rothman failed and refused to attend his noticed deposition repeatedly, thereby causing Michael Jackson's attorneys to file a motion to compel the deposition of Mr. Rothman, as well as request sanctions. Mr. Rothman claimed attorney/client privilege as his basis for not attending the noticed deposition. Michael Jackson's attorneys admonished him that he should have obtained a waiver of privilege before filing the within action, and that he should either obtain the waiver or dismiss the case.

On January 8, 1994, a Request for Judicial Notice was filed and set for hearing on February 2, 1994, concurrently with a Motion to Strike plaintiff's (Rothman's) second amended verified complaint. In a Stipulation re Taking Off Calendar Motion filed by Mr. Weitzman and Mr. Katten, the key points stated that Michael Jackson had already dismissed Mr. Weitzman and Mr. Katten from the case. It further stated that the Motion to Strike was not the most desirable vehicle to bring before the Court the parties' dispute regarding the meaning and intent of the Agreement. Mr. Weitzman & Mr. Katten recommended that Mr. Rothman should file a Motion for Leave to amend his Second Amended Verified Complaint if he wanted to name Mr. Weitzman and Mr. Katten as Doe defendants as the appropriate vehicle for presenting to the Court the parties' dispute. The Court granted the Motion to Compel

— REDEMPTION —

and ordered Mr. Rothman's deposition to be taken and sanctioned Mr. Rothman $850.00.

Under federal law, title 28, section 1927, Sanctions are imposed against lawyers for conduct that manifests either intentional or reckless disregard of the attorney's duties as officers of the Court. The Court examines whether counsel's conduct, when viewed objectively, imposed unreasonable and unwarranted burdens on the Court and opposing parties, and whether counsel acted recklessly or with indifference to the law.

Part 6
A Ram In The Bush

A Ram In The Bush

In Genesis 22:13, the Bible says, "...and behold, behind him a ram caught in a thicket by his horns..."

Immediately after leaving Mr. Rothman's employment I could not understand why I got caught in the midst of the thicket of this entire situation. It felt like I was between a rock and a hard place. On the one hand, I felt I had been exposed to the greatest acts of deception in a profession I loved. On the other hand, in order to come forth with this book I had to reveal errors in the legal profession that I loved and in which I enjoyed a 20-year work history.

At the onset of the child molestation investigation I attempted to assist the investigation by coming forth with the same information that I am revealing in this book. However, when the case settled, all the information that I provided went nowhere. Since the settlement resolved all the pertinent issues between the parties involved in the Civil case, there was still the issue concerning the extortion case that was never resolved; just dismissed.

In 1997, while attending a music conference, a freelance editor from Simon Schuster came to encourage anyone that had a good idea to consider writing a book about it. I thought it was strange that an editor would be at a gospel music conference. It wasn't until I returned home that the idea to write a book about this entire incident really took root in my soul. The thought of writing a book had not previously crossed my mind. When I provided the information revealed in this book to the investigators, I was only interested in seeing justice served.

Not knowing what my first move should be, other than writing the book, I decided I wanted to at least contact someone that could make Michael Jackson aware of my intentions, because it would involve revisiting this incident, and I wanted to at least be respectful of his feelings. I did not know how to locate him, but remembered that his mother and father lived on Havenhurst in Encino. I wrote a letter addressed to Katherine & Joseph Jackson, advising them who I was and what I was about to do and asked them, in the letter, to please call me with their comments concerning the project.

I drove to Havenhurst looking for their residence so I could put the letter in their mail box. Not knowing their exact address and hoping to recognize the house from magazine pictures, I drove up and down Havenhurst from Ventura to the end. I must have driven for about one hour without finding anything that looked similar to the pictures I had seen of their residence.

Finally, I stopped in frustration and said a prayer. I was exhausted with the whole idea of trying to find a place by only a picture I had seen in a magazine and without knowing its actual physical location. All I had was a street name. I have, however, had that experience before, where I was led directly to an unknown target with the simple instructions, "just get in your car and drive." Well, I didn't quite get that same instruction this time. This time the instruction was to, "write the letter." I asked God in prayer, "if you want me to do this, you make it possible for me to give this letter to the Jackson family if it is your will." With the prayer said and done, I headed towards home. I felt assured that if this was God's will he would make a way known.

On my way home, within several minutes of praying that prayer, while stopped at a light on Van Nuys Blvd. in Sherman Oaks, I spotted a black Mercedes Benz stopped across the street, getting ready to make a left-hand turn. The driver of the car looked like Michael Jackson's mother, Katherine Jackson. I was astonished! God answered that prayer instantly. I turned around and pulled next to her car and my first words were, "this must be God." She was probably surprised when I handed her a letter already addressed to her and Joseph Jackson. I asked her to please read the letter and give me a call if she had any questions concerning it.

Shortly after giving her the letter I moved and my telephone number changed; therefore, I never knew if she tried to call me concerning the letter. I was convinced that I had accomplished the goal of at least informing the Jackson family about my mission to write the book.

It started to become very obvious to me that God's hand was moving me and guiding me in this book writing project. He gave me the idea, and allowed me to run into Katherine Jackson the very day I went looking for their residence. He also strategically put me in the midst of Mr. Rothman's office at such a crucial time to bear witness to the true facts surrounding that case.

When I began to research Michael Jackson's life, I discovered more humanitarian deeds than I had ever known and probably thousands more that are unknown. This reminds me of a Bible verse that says, "What you do to the least of mine, is as if you are doing it unto me." I cannot speak to the level of Michael Jackson's spirituality, but I do know that there is a divine force guiding him to help the world solve crucial issues that most people simply sit back and ignore. For those of you who can take the word of God as a guide, it says, "you judge a tree by the fruit that it bears. How can a tree be bad when it bears good fruit, and how can a tree be good, when it bears bad fruit?" Even in God's Holy Bible He says judge a man by his fruit, his works, his acts or deeds. Let his fruits, acts, deeds and works of his hand be your guide to know the heart of that man.

Michael Jackson's talent has transcended beyond color lines and cultures throughout the world. He has broken every music record in the entertainment industry. You name it, and Michael Jackson's talent has surpassed it. Some notable records broken by Michael Jackson and entered into the Guinness Book of World Records include:

Most successful concert series: Michael Jackson sold out for seven nights at Wembley Stadium, London, England in the summer of 1988. A total of 504,000 people saw Michael Jackson perform in July and August of 1988.

Biggest selling album of all time: Michael Jackson's *Thriller* album is the biggest selling album of all times, with over 50 million copies sold worldwide and over 25 million copies sold in the U.S.

80's most #1 hits: Michael Jackson had more #1 hits than any other artist for the decade.

Awards: Michael Jackson has more awards than any other artist.

Entertainer of the Decade: Michael Jackson was the entertainer of the world in 1980 with the #1 ranked albums of *Thriller* and *Bad*.

Most Grammy Awards: Michael Jackson won a record breaking 8 Grammy Awards in 1984, more than any other artist in one year.

Largest Contracts: Michael Jackson had the largest contract with Sony Music, 890 million dollars and earnings of one billion.

Greatest Audience: The highest ever viewership of 133.4 million viewers that watched the NBC transmission of the Super Bowl XXVII on June 31, 1993. Michael Jackson was spotlighted during the halftime performance.

Highest Paid Commercial Spokesman: Pepsi Cola paid Michael Jackson twelve million to do four TV commercials.

Bad Tour: Michael Jackson's world tour brought in a record gross revenue of over 124 million during September 1987 – December 1988.

100 Million Records: Michael Jackson has sold over 100 million singles and albums outside of the U.S.

Billboard Charts: Michael Jackson is the first person in the 37 year history of the charts to enter at #1 with his single *You Are Not Alone*.

Biggest seller video: Michael Jackson's *The Making of Thriller* was the biggest selling video to be released by an artist.

— REDEMPTION —

Billboard "Hot 100" Singles Chart: The most #1 hits by a male artist.

#1 Debuts: Michael Jackson's *Bad*, *Dangerous* and *History* albums all debuted at #1.

Consecutive #1 Singles: Jackson 5 were the first group to have four consecutive #1 singles.

#1 On Charts: In 1983, Michael Jackson became the first artist to simultaneously hold the number one spots on Billboards' rock albums and rock singles charts, as well as the R&B albums and singles charts.

First Video: Michael Jackson was the first black artist to have a video aired on MTV.

Michael Jackson's incredible talent has bridged the gap between young and old, male and female, white and black, across nations of the world. Incredible, thought provoking songs such as *Man In The Mirror*, which goes to the heart of changing the world by starting with the *Man In The Mirror* shed light on Michael Jackson's desire to see a better world. His inspiring song, *We Are The World*, which was recorded by various hit artists encouraging the world to start giving to help make the world a better place. His music spoke directly to social issues, social change and encouraged others to help make the world a better place.

This book brings leverage from a different source into the child molestation allegations. This whole case started with the accusations of one boy. Now, with the witness of one, I bring the truth about the child molestation allegations witnessed from another side. They crucified Michael Jackson's character, assassinated his reputation, accused him falsely, nailed him on the cross with vicious lies, and robbed him of his earthly goods.

I might be wrong, but he **does not** sound like your typical pedophile, someone looking to hurt a child, but instead sounds like someone who has vision for world peace. Helping mankind by starting with *the man in the mirror*.

With all of Michael Jackson's notoriety, awards, millions of dollars, record breaking statistics and fans all over the world, he remains surprisingly humble, meek, unselfish, always caring for world unity, dying children, underprivileged children and reaching out to a hurting world. He never publicly broadcasted his humanitarian acts and deeds because of meekness and humility.

Instead of using his millions on drugs, alcohol, women and gambling, he has chosen to live an impeccable life in the public's eyes. In the movie, *The Jackson's American Dream*, Michael Jackson was upset when his brother got married. His statement was, "you are disappointing our fans." It is my guess, that his desire to be single and live unmarried before this incident stemmed from his wanting all his adoring fans to have a symbolic piece of him, fulfilling their fantasies to the fullest by his remaining single, available and free. Even his stage performance and presence seduces his audience with bodily gestures that portrays the sensual side of Michael Jackson.

Everyone that I have ever known who helps anyone underprivileged, such as children, women, seniors, homeless and the hungry, seems to have an incredible blessing on their lives. There seems to be a divine law in this universe that renders back to each individual on their giving. The advantage of having spiritual insight is that you are forewarned; therefore, you are forearmed. But even for those not aware, that principle works, whether you know it or not. Just like the law of gravity—it also works whether you know it or not. Whether you know what gravity is or is not, the instant you jump off a building gravity is right there to introduce itself as it pulls you down rapidly to the ground.

When you give kindness, kindness comes back. When you give love, love comes back. Likewise, when you give selfishness, life renders selfishness back to you. When you give deceit, murder, stealing, etc., life robs you of the same deceit you are giving, life murders your life, life steals your life and so on…. It takes some people their whole lifetime to find out, at the end, that they have just been living a big payback lifestyle.

On the other hand, if you are living successful and have played all the cards right, treating people right and acknowledging God as your source, it doesn't mean nothing bad will never happen to you in your lifetime. The difference in this scenario, is that because you have done good and treated people right and fair, right and fair comes to your rescue when you need it. If you're considerate, consideration comes to your aide when you need it. If you're kind,kindness comes to your side when you need it the most.

Don't be fooled by a person who treats people unfairly, thinking they are having a happy life, no matter what it looks like. Don't think that just because people don't get caught breaking the law that they are living a happy life.

I believe Michael Jackson has the favor of God on his life. For all the children Michael Jackson has helped, all the smiles that he has put on many faces, all the love he has extended to those in need, I believe God gave Michael Jackson a ram in the bush.

Part 7
Here And Now...

7.1 The Fans

Michael Jackson maintained loyal, devoted fans who supported him, encouraged him and showered him with their love and affection throughout the child molestation allegations. Polls were taken by mainstream media and it was determined that more than 65% said they would still buy Michael Jackson's music; 80% did not believe the allegations of child molestation; 70% did not believe the allegations would affect his career; and more than 76% said they believed Michael Jackson would maintain his status in the future.

The outpouring of support for Michael Jackson by his millions of fans around the world was overwhelming. Fans poured out their love and support for him through his many Websites, fan clubs, international clubs, and they continued to buy his products and attend his concerts in record numbers, even while the investigation was ongoing. All the love Michael Jackson gave to the world, his fans gave back to him by jamming phone lines to express their love and continued support for Michael Jackson; jamming into the stadiums in record numbers to show their support of his concerts. It was even reported that his fans surrounded his hotel during the *Dangerous Tour* singing *Heal The World*.

On Michael Jackson's 35th birthday in August, 1993, forty-seven thousand of his fans attended his concert, even with threats of monsoon rains. They showered him with love chants and sang happy birthday to him in the middle of the concert, moving Michael Jackson to tears. In spite of the cancellations and rescheduled tours, fans still showed up in record numbers. His fans supported him at his concerts with chants of , "We love you Michael!" Ninety-three thousand fans showed up in Moscow; Eighty thousand fans showed up in Tel Aviv, Jerusalem, thousands in Buenos Aires, Argentina where thousands of tickets were given away to underprivileged children. Seventy thousand fans poured into the Aztec Stadium in Mexico to show their support for Michael Jackson. They all shouted, "Michael, Michael!"

The fans continued to support his *Dangerous* album in excess of half a million copies in Mexico alone. His sales were increasing during the heart of the child molestation allegations launched against him. His performance in Buenos Aires, Argentina had a showing of two hundred and forty thousand fans; Sao Paulo, Brazil had a showing of one hundred and sixty thousand fans; and Santiago, Chile had a showing of eight-five thousand fans.

It was shortly after concluding his Mexico tour dates in November of 1993, that Michael Jackson released a statement announcing the end of his *Dangerous Tour*. He expressed the need to seek medical attention for dependency and treatment for addiction to painkillers. He also mentioned that because of the, "humiliation, embarrassment, hurt and shame... the pressure resulting from these false allegations coupled with the incredible energy necessary for me to perform caused so much distress that it left me physically and emotionally exhausted." The painkillers were prescribed to Michael Jackson after he had undergone treatment for the burn to his scalp while filming a Pepsi commercial.

Michael Jackson's long time friend, Elizabeth Taylor, was reported to have cancelled her tour to fly to Singapore to be by his side during this ordeal. She stated that she, "believed totally that Michael Jackson would be vindicated..." Also stating that she believed in his integrity, love and respect for children. She and her then husband, Larry Fortinsky, who had also recovered from a drug dependency years before, flew to Mexico to assist Michael Jackson in getting out of Mexico and getting treatment for his admitted drug dependency. Elizabeth Taylor's role of devoted friend was instrumental in helping Michael Jackson cope during this very difficult, highly public moment in his life. When the film industry called her the most beautiful lady in the industry, we all thought they were talking about her outer beauty. She demonstrated the real beauty of a person lies within. Her unwavering support of Michael Jackson in front of the world also demonstrated her loyalty as a friend. Elizabeth Taylor dropped her hectic schedule to be by Michael Jackson's side, giving him guidance and advice. Her courage and support of Michael Jackson during this ordeal helped me to realize that despite the viciousness that goes on in the world today, despite all the hate, injustice and prejudices, there are still decent human beings of all races who know the true meaning of love.

The Jackson family united in a press release stating their "...belief that Michael was being made the victim of a cruel and obvious attempt to take advantage of his fame and success... that he has dedicated his life to providing happiness to young people everywhere... Our entire family stands firmly at his side."

Many loyal friends publicly expressed their support for Michael Jackson during this ordeal by stating that Michael Jackson was, "incapable of hurting a child." Michael Jackson flew one of his fans, a 15 year old Dutch boy who was undergoing chemotherapy for cancer and his two brothers, to Japan to attend his concert. He was referred by the Make A Wish Foundation where the boy wished to meet Michael Jackson.

The loyal support of family, friends, fans and sponsors such as Sony Music and Pepsi, proved to the world that Michael Jackson is more than an entertainer. He represents hope, love, inspiration and joy to a world plagued with so much destitution, sickness, hunger and destruction. Michael Jackson said it all with his song, *We Are The World*. He kept millions of people aware of the need to help one another, starting with you and me, and to heal the world with love.

Michael Jackson's fans claim to know him through his music. They understand the heart of Michael Jackson by the lyrics of his songs. They know when he is hurting, disgusted, in pain and they hear his messages of anger at the media in songs like, *Leave Me Alone*. They heard his heart's cry for world peace and racial justice in songs like, *Black or White*, and embraced his antidote for changing the world by starting with *The Man In The Mirror*.

The allegation of child molestation by one boy whose father was hungry for money, not justice, was not enough to change the hearts of millions of Michael Jackson fans around the world. Michael Jackson's expression of love shown to children throughout the years has multiplied through the love of his fans.

The boy's father predicted that he would "destroy Michael Jackson... He won't sell another record..." and, "They will be destroyed forever," proved to be totally untrue. Dr. Chandler, in all his threats, could not break the bonds of love. When all the smoke clears and the dust settles, love always prevails over evil, and biblically speaking, "love will never fail."

7.2
Michael Moves On With His Life

Since the child molestation allegations and resulting legal battles, Michael Jackson has moved on with his life. As we all know, he also married Lisa Marie Presley and their marriage ended with their parting as friends. He then married his nurse, Debbie Rowe, in November 1996 and, for the first time, is the proud father of two beautiful children, Prince Michael, and Paris Michael Katherine, named after the French capital where she was conceived. It is reported that with the help of 24-hour nannies, he is raising his children and is called a *doting father*.

Michael Jackson has been sued on copyright infringement cases since the child molestation allegations, but has won them all. He was also victorious in the lawsuits brought by five of his former bodyguards and the sixty million dollar lawsuit brought in 1999 by Dr. Chandler, claiming Michael Jackson violated the confidentiality settlement by lyrics in his *Dangerous* song, *Jew Me Sue Me*.

Michael Jackson has managed to repair the damage to his reputation caused by the child abuse molestation allegations. He continued, even during the allegations, to support numerous charities. His love for helping underprivileged children never stopped. He kept a promise that he made to the citizens of Krindjabo during a visit to the Ivory Coast, West Africa in 1992, where he was crowned King of the Sanwis (an honor that has been given only to visiting dignitaries), to build a cultural center for the village.

Michael Jackson received a lot of support from the music industry. Record chain owners reported that Michael Jackson's album sales had, in fact, increased after the child abuse allegations. Even though radio listeners said they would continue to buy Michael Jackson's records and go to his concerts, as of this writing, Michael Jackson has not done a national concert in the United States since the child abuse allegations. It is apparent that his fans in the United States miss the incredible talent of the King of Pop. When he walked out on stage at the Jackson Family Honors which took place in February of 1994 at the MGM Grand Hotel in Las Vegas, the entire audience rose to their feet cheering, waiving, blowing kisses and shouting "I love you!" for over eight minutes. The audience was in an uproar!

As of September 1999, the six year statute of limitations has run out on the child molestation allegations. Although this case was concluded when the grand jury could not find enough credible evidence to indict Michael Jackson, it is officially over and Michael Jackson is moving on with his life.

Part 8
Afterword

Afterword

In a statement issued by Michael Jackson in December of 1993, just a few months after the child molestation allegations, he said, "...Throughout my life I have only tried to help thousands upon thousands of children to live happy lives. It brings tears to my eyes when I see any child who suffers. If I am guilty of anything, it is of believing what God said about children: 'Suffer the little children to come unto me, and forbid them not: for of such is the Kingdom of God.' [Mark 10:14] In no way do I think that I am God, but I do try to be God-like in my heart."

As mentioned in the beginning, the Bible says that you, "judge a tree by the fruit that it bears." Michael Jackson's words, his deeds, his actions and his lifestyle all validate who he really is behind the scenes. No matter how hard the media and tabloids try to portray him as something other than who he really is, Michael Jackson's past and present actions speak for themselves.

There are millions of Christians who live a chaste life without drugs or alcohol. Who in turn give back to society, with gratefulness and thanksgiving, in return for what God has given them, eternal life. There are not many individuals with millions to give, like Michael Jackson, but collectively Christians help feed the poor all over the world. They, too, are on a mission from God — being commissioned to give to others like God gave Jesus, His very own Son, for our salvation.

Michael Jackson's mission here on earth extends beyond being the greatest entertainer of all times, greater than feeding the poor. It is obvious from his actions and deeds that his mission is to help promote world peace. He uses his icon status and influence to spread love and the message of world peace, and effectively brings down walls of division between races. His music sells throughout the world by young, old, white, black, brown, rich, poor, male and female. He brings the message of love, unity, and world peace to this generation through the next generation of children; the ones that will carry the torch into the future. Offsetting the message of hate, violence, evil and despair that has been infiltrated from the beginning of time throughout the world; only on the platform of love can the people of the world truly be united. Hate causes division, separatism, alienation, divorce and isolation.

A revelation came to me while completing this book, and that is that the real set-up behind the scenes of the Michael Jackson child molestation allegations goes deeper than Dr. Chandler, Mr. Rothman, the media and tabloids. It is my belief that at the center of this entire scheme was the work of a demonic force to abort Michael Jackson's purpose and cry for world peace. We all have a destiny and a purpose for being created. We fail to reach our creative destiny in life because of ignorance, stupidity and sabotage. In Michael Jackson's case, you could say sabotage threatened him from reaching his destiny. I believe Michael Jackson was consciously using his icon status to bring people all across the world together in peace. A purpose that could have only come from God — the Creator of this universe.

Some people among the Black Race contend that there is a conspiracy to bring down black superstars. Although I do not discard this contention completely, I believe there is a strong demonic force on this earth that tries to equally destroy anyone fighting this same cause and to bridge the gap for humanity and promote world peace between the races, or equality for all mankind. Killing the messenger is still a popular tactic used over and over by the evil ruler of this universe, known to most Biblically as Satan...

There is obviously something very evil embedded in the core of this society that has brought death and destruction to so many races of people by keeping us divided, an evil that not only does not want to see unity among the races, but also attempts to destroy another race because they believe themselves to be the superior race, (Ethnocentrism). The truth is that Satan is the demonic force in this world. He cannot operate without willing vessels. He uses greed, power, lust, jealousy, anger and unforgiveness, just to name a few, as his luring devices and techniques. There is a saying that, "whatever things you do, that spirit will come and live in you."

Like Reverend Jesse Jackson once said, "keep hope alive!" I encourage the readers of this book to continue to strive to make this world a better place. Michael Jackson stated in his song, *We Are The World*. "The day is drawing near when all evil will be dealt with and evildoers will have their place in Hell for eternity." This is true whether you believe it or not, whether you acknowledge it or not.

The day is coming soon when everyone will give an account for their deeds done on this earth. Whether you are part of the media, a politician, a dentist, attorney, in a gang, a drug dealer, an addict, a prostitute, fornicator, adulterer, child molester, murderer, thief, rapist, sexual deviant, a racist, and/or have committed any other acts of darkness or anyone that violates the laws of God, you will be required to stand before the throne of God, Creator of the universe, and be judged according to your deeds.

The good news is that forgiveness is available for everyone just for the asking. No matter what you have done or who you are, whether Jewish, Buddhist, Catholic, Jehovah's Witness, Baptist, Pentecostal, AME, Atheist, etc., Jesus' blood was shed for you to be forgiven for all your deeds while you are yet breathing. No deed is too devious for the cleansing blood of Jesus. Whether you believe in God or not, the blood of Jesus was shed for you. In fact, if you don't believe this to be true, just trust God and receive it for yourself.

It is my prayer that the Chandler family, Mr. Rothman, and anyone else who participated in this case, and is aware of any wrongdoing, would have the courage to come forth in truthfulness with a repentant heart. Only the truth will set you free, and salvation is gained through repentance. The definition of *repent* is to, turn from sin and dedicate oneself to the amendment of one's life... To change one's mind. Hell was not designed for man. It was designed for Satan and his demonic host.

I also would like to urge the then 13-year old Chandler boy to come forth and tell the truth of what really happened. It's time for healing and closure in this case. Although this case started out with a lot of hype, accusations, media coverage and investigations, everyone knows pretty much that the real truth has not yet been told. Your courage will set an innocent person free and the blessings of God will follow you for the rest of your life and into eternity. You cannot take anything from this life into eternity, only your deeds will stand before you and God.

Michael - The Humanitarian

Michael Jackson is known throughout the world as the: *most caring humanitarian*. It is no secret—the many charities, foundations and acts of love that Michael Jackson has shown throughout his life, especially for children who are underprivileged and disadvantaged. Michael Jackson's Heal The World Foundation, was founded in 1992 as a charitable organization to aid children and the environment. It provides medicine for children, fights world hunger, drug and alcohol abuse, and child abuse. Heal The World Foundation works with local and national organizations, sharing expertise in delivering services to disadvantaged children throughout the world.

Here are a few of the accomplishments of Heal The World Foundation:

In 1992:

June - Donated $100,000 DM to Children's Hospital in Rotterdam

July - Donated L. 821,477,296 to La Partita del Cuore (The Heart Match) in Rome. Donated 120,000 DM to children's charities in Estonia and Latvia.

September - Donated 1 million pesetas to a charity headed by the Queen of Spain. Donated children's playground at orphanage in Bucharest, Romania.

November - Forty-seven tons of winter relief supplies airlifted to children of Sarajevo in association with AmeriCares, including medical items, blankets, winter clothing and shoes.

December - Relief supplies airlifted to children in Bosnia in association with Operation Christmas Child, consisting of

30,000 *shoebox g*ifts of toys, school items, photographs, and letters collected by U.K school children.

In 1993:

January - A new U.S. Children's Relief Initiative announced in Los Angeles: Heal L.A. in collaboration with Cities In Schools, Big Brothers/Big Sisters, the BEST Foundation, Watts Health Foundation and the Partnership for Drug Free America, that it will help solve the problems facing inner-city youth by providing drug-abuse and AIDS prevention education, mentoring and immunization campaigns in the wake of the 1992 unrest.

Donated 1.25 million dollars plus proceeds from Michael Jackson's half-time performance at the Super Bowl XXVII in Pasadena, CA (USA) to Heal L.A.

February - In association with Sega, launched an initiative to distribute more than $108,000 of computer games and equipment to children's hospitals, children's homes, and children's charities throughout the U.K.

April - Unannounced visit made by Michael Jackson to three Heal L.A. project sites to participate in discussions with recipients and providers of the immunization, mentoring and drug-abuse prevention programs.

May - With the assistance of former U.S. President Jimmy Carter's Atlanta Project Immunization/Children's Health Initiative, arranged for the immunization of 17,000 children in 5 days in Atlanta, Ga.; support from Turner Broadcasting System, Inc., Ronald McDonald Children's Charities, Gladys Knight and TLC.

August - With Pepsi-Cola Thailand, donated $40,000 to Crown Princess Maha Chakri Sirindhorn's charity, the Rural School Children and Youth Development Fund, supporting school lunch programs in rural villages in Thailand.

In conjunction with Pepsi-Cola International, donated new ambulances to the Contacts One Independent Living Center for Children in Moscow, Russia and the Hospital de Ninos Dr. Ricardo Gutierrez in Buenos Aires, Argentina.

— REDEMPTION —

October - Donated $100,000 to the Children's Defense Fund, the Children's Diabetes Foundation, the Atlanta Project, and the Boys and Girls Clubs of Newark, New Jersey.

December - The Gorbachev Foundation airlifted 60,000 doses of children's vaccines to Tblisi, Georgia.

Operation Christmas Child gave to children in former Yugoslavia over 100,000 *shoebox gifts* of toys, small gifts and letters donated by children in the U.K.

In 1994:

January - In conjunction with Unihealth and the Los Angeles Immunization Coalition, vaccines were provided to children made homeless by the Los Angeles earthquake, with Discovery Toys donating hundreds of toys to the children in the immunization drive.

Eighty-five thousand dollars was provided through Heal L.A. to earthquake relief efforts by non-profit organizations dedicated to aiding families with long-term recovery, including the Al Wooten Jr. Heritage Center, Casa Rutilio Grande, Clinica Para Las Americas, Families in New Directions, Meeting Each Need With Dignity, Proyecto Esperanza, Pueblo Nuevo, and the Vaughn Street Family Center.

In association with General Electric, Lever Brothers, and Surf Wash, donated washers, dryers and soap to 25 non-profit organizations to provide free laundry services to families affected by the earthquake.

Heal the World L.A. board member Edward James Olmos provided education about earthquake safety to quake victims in shelters.

With the Salvation Army, treated over 400 homeless children and parents to a day at Universal Studios.

Spring-Summer: Heal L.A. Immunization and Mentoring Initiatives supported by visits by Kriss Kross to the George C. Page Children's Hospital Community Health Center and Raven Simone and Bryton McClure to the Bancroft Middle School.

Summer: In conjunction with the Los Angeles Unified School District, Youth Services, the I Have A Dream Foundation, Best Buddies, Overcoming Obstacles and California One to One, provided 2000 children with tickets to see Janet Jackson in concert, the "L.A. Laker Jam" and the Beach Boys.

August - In association with Toys "R" Us and AmeriCares, $20,000 worth of toys, food and supplies were distributed to children's hospital in Budapest, Hungary.

Fall - Heal L.A. funds distributed to Los Angeles Team Mentoring Program in six Los Angeles Unified School District Middle Schools in the South Central Los Angeles and the Pico Union District, reaching over 1000 young people.

October - A Community School/Safe Havens Initiative designed to provide Los Angeles communities with a safe environment for students, families and resident to pursue after-school academic and recreational activities such as instruction in computers, languages, mathematics and sports was launched.

In 1995:

February - Heal L.A. expanded curriculum offerings and program hours of the Community School/Safe Havens Initiative, which included over 1200 families.

March - Paid for liver transplant for young Hungarian boy, Bela Farkan.

April - Sponsored 46 children from 17 nations to gather at Neverland for the World Congress of Children, a three-day seminar to discuss drug abuse, homelessness, increasing violence, AIDS and child abuse.

June - Heal The World/World Children's Congress youth ambassadors presented the findings of the World Children's Congress to the World Summit of Children during the United Nations' 50th Anniversary celebration in San Francisco, CA, and met with U.N. Secretary Boutros-Ghali, the Rev. Jesse Jackson, Archbishop Desmond Tutu and several other U.N. ambassadors.

Summer - Heal the World/World Children's Congress youth ambassador from Mexico accompanies Children's Torch of Hope across the U.S. bringing the message of the World

— REDEMPTION —

Children's Congress to over 30 events sponsored by the Coalition for Children of the Earth and EC2000.

October - Brownstone and Tasha Scott perform at Horace Mann Middle School to launch new school year for Community School/Safe Havens Initiative.

Heal the World/World Children's Congress youth ambassadors report to the U.N. Committee on the Rights of the Child in Geneva, Switzerland.

December - Heal the World/World Children's Congress youth ambassadors address the dedication of the "Guardians of the Future" monument in Mexico City, co-sponsored by EC2000, Terra Christa Communications, UNICEF, the office of the mayor of Mexico City, and Coalition for Children of the Earth.

In association with the International Rescue Committee, shipped two pallets of toys to children in war-scarred Bosnia and Hercegovina.

In 1996:

February - Heal the World/World Children's Congress youth ambassador from Mexico presented model for creating a sustainable environment to the U.N. Habitat II Prep Committee.

April - Heal The World/World Children's Congress youth ambassadors attended Children First: A Global Forum in Atlanta, Georgia. The event, hosted by former U.S. President Jimmy Carter, Rosalyn Carter, the Carter Center and the Task Force for Child Survival, co-sponsored by the Rockefeller Foundation, the Annie E. Casey Foundation, the World Bank, and Heal the World, brings together 360 representatives from 100 countries to discuss strategies to improve the quality of life for children.

Heal the World/World Children's Congress youth ambassadors attended the Spectrum of Light Youth Conference in Washington, D.C. to form partnerships emphasizing the need for a sustainable society based on a healthy environment.

— Geraldine Hughes —

Just to name a few... Michael Jackson's humanitarian efforts started long before the child molestation allegations surfaced, and continued even through the most difficult time of his life. He did not allow his suffering and pain to interfere with his continued efforts to help hurting children all around the world.

Humanitarian: A person promoting human welfare and social reform.

Appendix

Spiritually Speaking

The Bible clearly commands us, "thou shall not bear false witness." That means you should not accuse your brother falsely. There is a special commandment that kicks into place if you are guilty of accusing your brother falsely, especially if that person belongs to God as His dear child. He (God) warns us that: "Whosoever shall offend one of these little ones that believe in me, it is better for him that a millstone were hanged about his neck, and he were cast into the sea." [Mark 9:42] The scriptures continue with, "...it is better for thee to enter into life (heaven) maimed, than having two hands to go into hell, into the fire that never shall be quenched: Where the worm dieth not, and the fire is not quenched. [Mark 9:43-44]

The fires of Hell are real. Anyone who breaks the laws of God is in eminent danger of its fires. There is no need to sweeten the blow of this reality, especially in light of blatant disregard for human rights.

"What profits a man to gain the whole world and lose his soul." No amount of money in the entire universe should be worth the fires of hell. There is nothing that money can buy that can be taken with us when we leave this earth. All we will be able to carry with us is our soul and the deeds that we have done in the flesh will be judged.

I am saying this to say, that if my convictions are being truly stated, which they are, and Michael Jackson was indeed falsely accused of molesting the boy, this is an opportunity for all involved to confess and say so. My writing this book does not undo any amount of damage already done by the false accusation concerning these allegations. It requires the parties to find a place in their heart where they can muster up enough courage to set an innocent man free by stepping up to the plate and admitting their guilt. No man or woman is perfect. We all fall short and mess up on a daily basis. What God looks for is how we handle those mess ups when they occur. Regardless of what you have heard about God, He is a God of second chances, and only in Him are we able to wipe our slate clean and start all over again.

I encourage all parties involved in this case to come forth and give God an opportunity to show Himself as a forgiving God. There is someone else, who will remain nameless, that knows what I am reporting here is true. I employ you to come forth and repent! By telling the truth I guarantee that you will not suffer anything as enormous as the lake of fire.

To anyone else not involved in this case who would like to know God as their personal Lord and savior, please repeat this prayer:

The prayer of salvation:

"Dear Jesus, come into my life. Forgive me for all my sins. Cleanse me of all unrighteousness. I believe you died for my sins. I believe you died and rose again on the third day and are seated at the right hand of God. Come into my heart and be my Savior. Dear God, receive me as your precious child. Holy Spirit, lead me guide me, direct my steps all the days of my life, in Jesus name I pray, Amen!"

If you want to be forgiven for all your sins, no matter what the issues are, pray this prayer with sincerity and the promise of eternal life in heaven will be yours the minute you conclude this prayer. Afterwards, pray daily, study the Bible and learn about the things of God. The Spirit of God will be able to direct you from that moment forward.

Choose you this day who you will serve, the creator of this universe, or the creature Satan?

* * *

— REDEMPTION —

Scripture references for my spiritual position and comments.

For there is nothing hid, which shall not be manifested, neither was any thing kept secret but that it should come abroad. [Mark 4:22]

What profits a man to gain the whole world, and lose his own soul. [Mark 8:36]

We all will go before the throne of God and give an account for our actions.

Whoso (ever) shall offend one of these little ones which believe in me, it is better for him that a millstone were hanged about his neck, and that he were drowned in the depth of the sea. [Matthew 18:6]

No man can serve two masters: for either he will hate the one, and love the other; or else he will hold to the one, and despise the other. Ye cannot serve God and mammon. [Matthew 6:24]

Blessed are the pure in heart, for they shall see God.

Blessed are the peacemakers, for they shall be called the children of God.

Blessed are they which are persecuted for righteousness sake, for theirs is the Kingdom of Heaven.

Blessed are you when men shall revile you, and persecute you, and shall say all manner of evil against you falsely, for my sake... Rejoice and be exceedingly glad, for great is your reward in heaven, for so persecuted they the prophets which were before you.

Ye are the salt of the earth... Ye are the light of the world... Let your light shine before men, that they may see your good works, and glorify your Father which is in heaven. [Matthew 5:8-16]

A good man out of the good treasure of his heart bringeth forth that which is good... An evil man out of the evil treasure of his heart bringeth forth that which is evil. [Luke 6:45]

Excerpts from Geraldine Hughes' 1993 Calendar Diary

08-09-93 Pellicano met at Rothman's office.

08-13-93 Pellicano met at Rothman's office. Dr. Chandler advised Rothman to file documents or he would fire him.

08-17-93 Ex Parte hearing filed by June Schwartz (June Chandler) to have her 13 year old son returned to her custody and the stipulation overturned.

08-17-93 Dr. Chandler took his son to see the psychiatrist who reported the allegations against Michael Jackson.

08-19-93 Mr. Freeman meets with Mr. Rothman.

08-23-93 Allegations of child sexual abuse against Michael Jackson hit the news media.

08-24-93 Dr. Chandler, Mr. Freeman, June Schwartz and David Schwartz met with Mr. Rothman for three hours in his office. I heard Dr. Chandler say, "I almost had a twenty million dollar deal."

08-26-93 Dr. Chandler and his 13-year old son were in Mr. Rothman's office all day. I heard Dr. Chandler say, "It's my

— REDEMPTION —

ass that's on the line and in danger of going to prison."

08-27-93 Dr. Chandler was in Mr. Rothman's office overnight.

08-28-93 I met with investigator Mr. Pellicano regarding statements.

08-30-93 Covertly made audio tape released by Mr. Pellicano of conversation between Dr. Chandler and David Schwartz.

09-01-93 Covertly made audio tape released by Mr. Pellicano of conversation between Mr. Rothman and Mr. Pellicano.

09-01-93 Dr. Chandler replaces his attorney, Mr. Rothman, with Mr. Hirsch.

09-14-93 The attorney for the 13-year old boy files lawsuit against Michael Jackson in court.

Excerpts From the Recorded Telephone Conversation Between Dr. Chandler and Mr. Dave Schwartz

Chandler: "I had a good communication with Michael. We were friends. I liked him and I respected him and everything else for what he is. There was no reason why he had to stop calling me. I sat in the room one day and talked to Michael and told him exactly what I want out of this whole relationship. I've been rehearsed about what to say and what not to say."

Schwartz: "What has Jackson done that made you so upset?"

Chandler: "He broke up the family. The boy has been seduced by this guy's power and money."

Chandler: "I am prepared to move against Michael Jackson. It's already set. There are other people involved that are waiting for my phone call that are in certain positions. I've paid them to do it. Everything's going according to a certain plan that isn't just mine. Once I make that phone call, this guy is going to destroy everybody in sight in any devious, nasty, cruel way that he can do it. And I've given him full authority to do that."